TEXTBOOK OF PROSTHETIC REHABILITATION IN PEDIATRIC DENTISTRY

A COMPLETE GUIDE OF PROSTHESIS

DR. ANKUR JAIN | DR. ANKITH MOHAN

Contents

CHAPTER I

INTRODUCTION

Pediatric dentistry is an integral part of the daily practice in dentistry. As in regular practice for adults, pediatric dentistry can be divided into several categories such as surgery, conservative dentistry or prosthetic. All these are most often linked together. Although less common than in adults, the pediatric prosthesis should not be excluded from child's dental treatment, which is often the case. In fact, dental care for children is not only limited to conservative dentistry, especially when the tooth is largely broken or even lost. Moreover, in some cases, the dentist is led to achieve prosthesis on children with large syndromes. Like the conventional prosthesis, the pediatric prosthesis has different forms: removable prosthesis and fixed prosthesis

Prosthodontic rehabilitation is possible and necessary in childhood as in adulthood, mostly in cases of premature tooth loss. Every tooth loss before it's a physiological shedding, and/or congenital absence of teeth may cause dysfunctions of the orofacial system, carrying several other complications from the functional, esthetic and psychological point of view. If deciduous teeth are lost prematurely, dentures will keep the space needed for permanent teeth growth and maintain regular jaw development.

In rare cases, the child may lose all its teeth because of progressive caries-related decay, injury or genetic imperfections. In clinical practice prosthetic reconstruction in children is mainly applied in patients with diseases associated with hypodontia and anodontia as a concomitant symptom, that is the phenotypic spectrum of associated malformations. Rarely undertaken in foudroyant tooth decay, mostly early childhood caries (ECC). Even though this type of therapy is not applied often, a temporary prosthesis may partly restitute lost function.

Application of removable dentures in children requires special attention, multidisciplinary approach and wide knowledge of the treatment planning and possibilities of reconstruction. Limited number of articles related to prosthetics in children and the author's long-standing clinical practice, confirm the insufficient clinical applicability of this type of therapy. The goal of prosthetic rehabilitation in children is to restore orofacial functions and normal occlusal relationships; this balance is essential to the proper conduct of the growth in children.[1]

The objective of this study, through a literature review, is to deepen the dentist's knowledge about the denture in children, its specificities, tooth loss etiology in temporary denture, the multiple prosthetic treatments and their indication. This work highlights the importance of an early management of tooth loss in order to avoid all kinds of complications

CHAPTER II

DEVELOPMENT OF PRIMARY TOOTH

The development of primary teeth begins while the baby is in the womb. At about 5 weeks' gestation, the first buds of primary teeth appear in the baby's jaws. At birth, the baby has a full set of 20 primary teeth (10 in the upper jaw, 10 in the lower jaw) and first permanent molar hidden under the gums. Primary teeth are also known as baby teeth, milk teeth or deciduous teeth.

1. DEVELOPMENT OF PRIMARY TOOTH

Tooth development or odontogenesis is the complex process by which teeth form from embryonic cell, grow, and erupt into the mouth. For human teeth to have a healthy oral environment, all parts of the tooth must develop during appropriate stages of foetal development. Primary teeth (baby teeth) start to form between the sixth and eighth week of prenatal development, and permanent teeth begin to form in the twentieth week. If teeth do not start to develop at or near these times, they will not develop at all, resulting in hypodontia or anodontia.

The tooth germ is an aggregation of cells that eventually forms a tooth. These cells are derived from the ectoderm of the first pharyngeal arch and the ectomesenchyme of the neural crest. The tooth germ is organized into three parts: the enamel organ, the dentalpapilla and the dental sac or follicle.

The *enamel organ* is composed of the outer enamel epithelium, inner enamelepithelium, stellate reticulum and stratum intermedium(fig no 1). These cells give rise to ameloblasts, which produce enamel and become a part of the reduced enamelepithelium (REE) after maturation of the enamel. The location where the outer enamel epithelium and inner enamel epithelium join is called the cervical loop. The growth of cervical loop cells into the deeper tissues forms Hertwig Epithelial Root Sheath, which determines the root shape of the tooth. During tooth development there are strong similarities between keratinization and amelogenesis. Keratin is also present in epithelial cells of tooth germ and a thin film of keratin is present on a recently erupted tooth (Nasmyth's membrane or enamel cuticle).[2]

The *dental papilla* contains cells that develop into odontoblasts, which are dentin- forming cells. Additionally, the junction between the dental papilla and inner enamel epithelium determines the crown shape of a tooth. Mesenchymal cells within the dental papilla are responsible for formation of tooth pulp.

The *dental sac or follicle* gives rise to three important entities: cementoblasts, osteoblasts, and fibroblasts. Cementoblasts form the cementum of a tooth. Osteoblasts give rise to the alveolar bone around the roots of teeth. Fibroblasts are involved developing the periodontal ligament which connect teeth to the alveolar bone through cementum. [2]

Stages

1. **Bud Stage**

This first stage happens at the eighth week in utero. At this time, cells known as dental epithelium bud from a thick band of cells called the dental lamina, which forms inside the upper and lower jaws. These cells will eventually evolve to form the tooth germ, which is made up of all the soft tissues necessary to grow a tooth.(Fig. 2)

2. Cap Stage

During this stage, cells begin to shape the outside layer of the tooth, forming a cap that sits on the rest of the tooth bud. This cap is called the enamel organ because it will later form the cells that produce enamel. The rest of the tooth bud, known as the dental papilla, will make the two interior layers of the tooth: the dentin and the pulp.[2]

Another sac of cells, called the dental follicle, surrounds both the enamel organ and the dental papilla. This sac contains blood vessels and nerves. By the cap stage, three different structures make up the tooth germ: the enamel organ, the dental papilla and the dental follicle.

3. **Bell Stage**

At this point, the enamel organ grows into a bell shape, and two events take place. First, cells of the enamel organ differentiate, meaning they change functions. Depending on their new function, they will fall into one of four cell groups:

- Inner enamel epithelium
- Outer enamel epithelium
- Stratum intermedium

- Stellate reticulum

Together, these cell groups work to develop the enamel layer of the tooth. During the second event in this stage, the enamel epithelium folds into the future shape of the tooth crown, and the dental lamina starts to break down. [2]

DENTAL GROWTH AND DEVELOPMET TIME

Dental Growth and Development

Primary Dentition						
	Calcification begins at	Formation complete at	Eruption		Exfoliation	
			Maxillary	Mandibular	Maxillary	Mandibular
Central incisors	4th fetal mo	18-24 mo	6-10 mo	5-8 mo	7-8 y	6-7 y
Lateral incisors	4th fetal mo	18-24 mo	8-12 mo	7-10 mo	8-9 y	7-8 y
Canines	4th fetal mo	30-39 mo	16-20 mo	16-20 mo	11-12 y	9-11 y
First molars	4th fetal mo	24-30 mo	11-18 mo	11-18 mo	9-11 y	10-12 y
Second molars	4th fetal mo	36 mo	20-30 mo	20-30 mo	9-12 y	11-13 y

Permanent Dentition					
	Calcification begins at	Crown (enamel) complete at	Roots complete at	Eruption*	
				Maxillary	Mandibular
Central incisors	3-4 mo	4-5 y	9-10 y	7-8 y (3)	6-7 y (2)
Lateral incisors	Maxilla: 10-12 mo	4-5 y	11 y	8-9 y (5)	7-8 y (4)
	Mandible: 3-4 mo	4-5 y	10 y		
Canines	4-5 mo	6-7 y	12-15 y	11-12 y (11)	9-11 y (6)
First premolars	18-24 mo	5-6 y	12-13 y	10-11 y (7)	10-12 y (8)
Second premolars	24-30 mo	6-7 y	12-14 y	10-12 y (9)	11-13 y (10)
First molars	Birth	30-36 mo	9-10 y	5.5-7 y (1)	5.5-7 y (1a)
Second molars	30-36 mo	7-8 y	14-16 y	12-14 y (12)	12-14 y (12a)
Third molars	Maxilla: 7-9 y			17-30 y (13)	17-30 y (13a)
	Mandible: 8-10 y				

Table no. 1

DEVELOPMENT OF PRIMARY TOOTH

The first tooth to come in is usually a middle front tooth on the lower jaw. This is called the central incisor. This is followed by the second central incisor on the lower jaw. Next, the 4 upper incisors usually come in. This is followed by the first 4 molars, and the remaining bottom 2 lateral incisors. Lateral incisors are beside (lateral to) the central incisors. Next, the 4 first molars come in. Then the cuspids, or the pointed teeth, appear.

Often, after the child reaches 2 years old, the 4 second molars (the last of the baby teeth) appear. The teeth on the upper jaw often erupt 1 to 2 months after the same tooth on the lower jaw. There are a total of 20 primary teeth. Often, about 1 tooth comes in per month once the teeth start coming in. There is normally a space between all the baby teeth. This leaves room for the larger permanent teeth to erupt.

The eruption sequence can vary quite a bit from child to child. So don't be too concerned if your child's teeth don't follow the pattern above. But if teeth fail to come in a year after the expected time, check with your child's dentist. He or she can to make sure the teeth are developing properly. Below is a chart showing average ages when teeth come in and fall out (are shed):

2. **OCCLUSION**

The primary dentition is complete with the eruption of the second primary molars, which means that the location for eruption of the permanent teeth in the future has already been determined at this stage. The dental arch circumference that connects the most distal surfaces of the right and left second primary molars should be preserved for the permanent dentition after the exchange of primary teeth. The relation between the distal surfaces of the maxillary and mandibular second primary molars is, therefore, one of the most important factors that influence the future occlusion of the permanent dentition.[3]

A-MESIAL STEP : -The distal surface of lower primary second molar is ahead or mesial to distal surface of upper primary second molar in centric occlusion is called as mesial step.(fig.1)

B-DISTAL STEP: - The distal surface of lower primary second molar is behind or distal to upper primary second molar in centric occlusion is called as distal step

C-FLUSH TERMINAL: - Flush terminal plane: When the distal surfaces of the upper and lower second primary molars were in the same vertical plane in centric occlusion

The occlusion of primary dentition can guide the eruption of permanent dentition

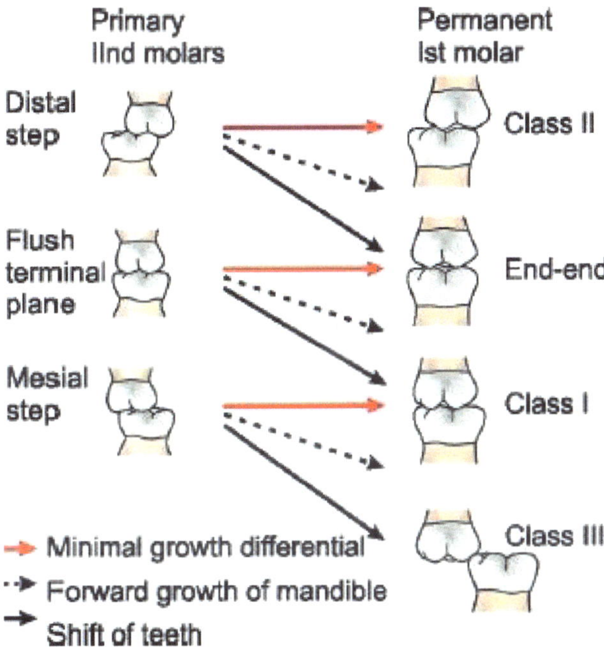

Fig. 1

Primary canine relationship: The relationship of primary maxillary and mandibular canine is one among the most stable occlusion in primary dentition

Class 1 – The primary canine interdigitates in the embrasure of maxillary laterals and canine

SPACING:-

- Delabarre in 1918 was the first to describe interdental spacing in primary dentition.
- Baume in 1950 divided the primary dentition into two parts, i.e. spaced and nonspaced. He also concluded that primary spacing occurs around

70 percent in maxilla and 63 percent in mandible.

- Joshi and Makhija (1984) found out that more amount of primary teeth spacing in males than in females.
- White and Gardiner (1976) reported that failure of incisor spacing occurs in 20 percent of cases before 5 years of age and usually indicated crowding in the permanent dentition.
- Foster and Hamilton (1969) reported that only 1 percent of British children had no space.

Spaced dentition: It is supposed to be good, as spaces in between the teeth can be utilized for adjustment of permanent successors, which are always larger in size compared to the deciduous teeth.

The spaces present are of two types

1. Primate spaces Exist between the maxillary lateral incisors and the canines (present mesial to maxillary deciduous canines) and mandibular canines and 1ˢᵗ deciduous molars (present distal to mandibular deciduous canines). These spaces are also called as anthropoid or simian spaces as they were initially found in our ancestral simian species.
2. Physiologic spaces Present in between all the primary teeth and play an important role in normal development of the permanent dentition. The total space present may vary from 0 to 8 mm with the average 4 mm in the maxillary arch and 1 to 7 mm with the average of 3 mm in the mandibular arch.
3. Nonspaced dentition this dentition is highlighted by lack of space between primary teeth either due to small jaw or larger teeth. This type of dentition usually indicates to crowding in developing permanent dentition.

3. SELF CORRECTING ANOMALIES OF PRIMARY AND MIXED DENTITION

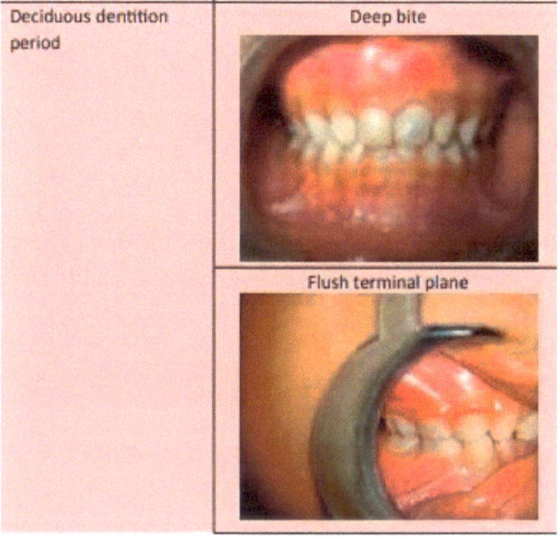

Fig no.2

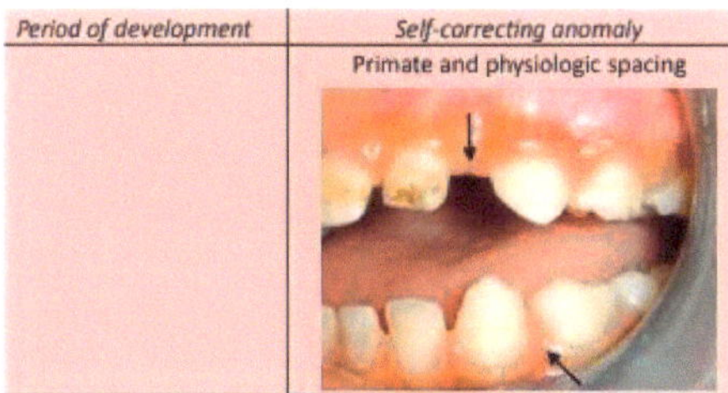

Fig no. 3

MIXED DENTITION

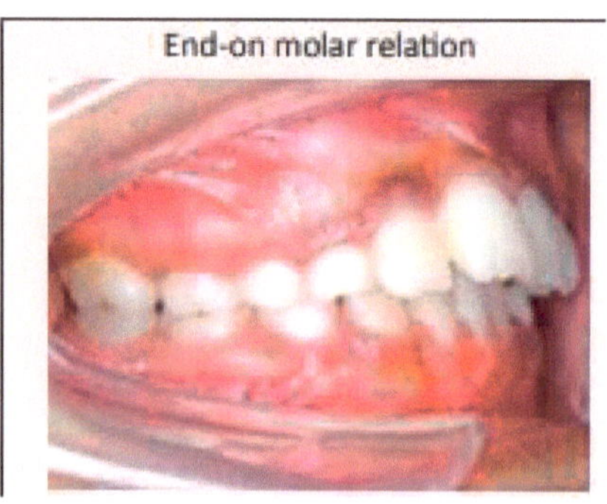

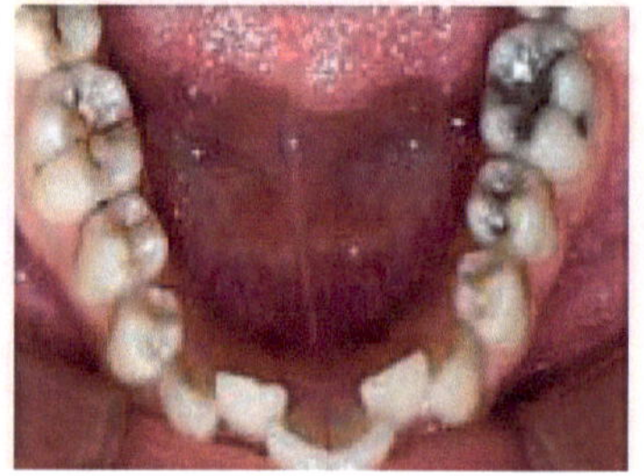

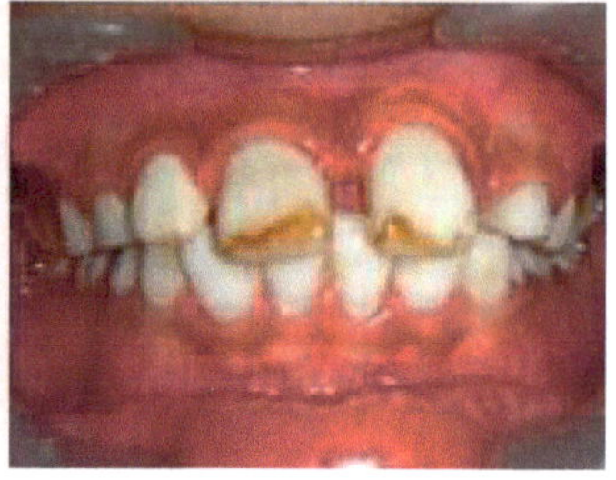

Fig no.4

4. PRESHEEDING OF PRIMARY TOOTH

Children typically begin shedding their primary teeth at the age of 6 years, starting with the central incisors and followed about a year later by the lateral incisors. The first molars are shed next, closely followed by the lower canines. The upper canines and both upper and lower second molars are shed last.(fig.5)

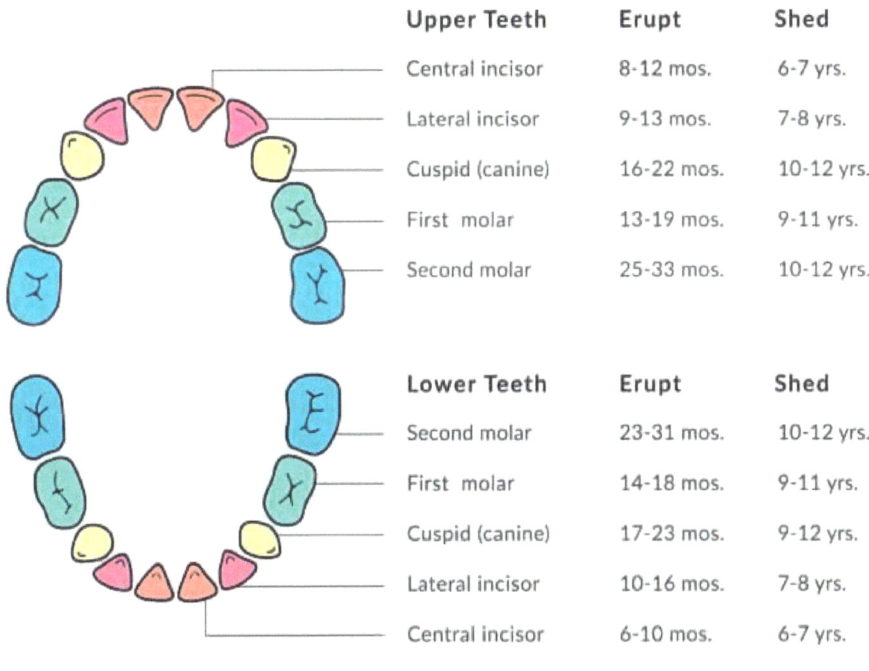

Upper Teeth	Erupt	Shed
Central incisor	8-12 mos.	6-7 yrs.
Lateral incisor	9-13 mos.	7-8 yrs.
Cuspid (canine)	16-22 mos.	10-12 yrs.
First molar	13-19 mos.	9-11 yrs.
Second molar	25-33 mos.	10-12 yrs.

Lower Teeth	Erupt	Shed
Second molar	23-31 mos.	10-12 yrs.
First molar	14-18 mos.	9-11 yrs.
Cuspid (canine)	17-23 mos.	9-12 yrs.
Lateral incisor	10-16 mos.	7-8 yrs.
Central incisor	6-10 mos.	6-7 yrs.

Fig no.5

PREMATURE LOSS OF PRIMARY TOOTH

Early tooth loss or premature exfoliation of teeth is defined as the loss of teeth in the oral cavity before the normal expected period. Both local and systemic factors can contribute to this phenomenon. Premature tooth loss can occur as a consequence of dental trauma, neonatal tooth extraction, early childhood caries, or periodontal problems, or it can be a manifestation of systemic disease. The most common causes of premature tooth loss are dental caries and trauma.

Premature loss of primary teeth can cause orthodontic problems such as crowding, ectopic eruption, or tooth impaction, which can result in malocclusion. It can also affect children's phonation, causing speech distortion. Psychosocial problems can also arise from premature tooth loss in children, especially when the child loses anterior teeth. Although younger children may not understand how missing a tooth affects their quality of life, some of them may feel unattractive in comparison to other children.

CHAPTER III

DENTURE IN CHILDREN

Dentures for kids are **a necessity if they are missing teeth due to ectodermal dysplasias**. The National Foundation for Ectodermal Dysplasias (NFED) has always advocated for dentures at a young age to replace their missing teeth

By now, your kids are either back to school or sitting at their work stations at home learning virtually. The National Foundation for Ectodermal Dysplasias (NFED) *strongly* encourages that children have and wear dentures before they start school, meaning pre-kindergarten or kindergarten.

Why do we take this stand and why is this so important for your child? Here are seven reasons.

Benefits of Dentures for Kids

1. **Improved jaw development and tissue development around the mouth.**

2. **Improved esthetics/appearances** – Dentures will create an age-appropriate facial appearance. The children do not have the "old man" appearance resulting from over closure of the jaws.

3. **Improved social well-being** – The children are happy and smiles instead of frowning, For the most part, their mouth looks like their peers. All of their friends have teeth! Kids want to fit in.

4. **Improved psychological well-being** – Children will feel better about themselves and as a result, will exhibit more self-confidence. Small children affected with an obvious physical deformity, such as the lack of teeth, run the risk of low self-esteem.

5. **Improved nutrition** – Digestion begins when you put food in your mouth. Chewing is an important to digestion and nutrition. If children can't chew, they can't eat all of the healthy, yummy foods that are available.

6.**Improved speech development** – Teeth greatly improve speech and increase vocabulary and communicative skills. This makes it easier for children to communicate with their friends and family and share their ideas and thoughts with everyone.

7. **Psychological uplift to the entire family** – By improving the child's appearance, you provide for a more normal physical development and you enhance better social and emotional adjustment. Your child and your entire family will rejoice in wearing dentures successfully!

Problems do and will arise. However, in most instances, you can overcome these hurdles through a cooperative effort between you, your child and the dentist. It requires teamwork! Be persistent with both your dentist and your child.[4]

A-EVOLUTION OF DENTURE IN CHILDREN I-PRIMARY DENTURE

The primary denture consists of twenty teeth distributed in four quadrants of five teeth each: two incisors, one canine and two molars per quadrants. [5]

Around the age of two years, all primary teeth have erupted. This state will last until the age of 6 years. These teeth will be functional for three to four years until the appearance of the first permanent molar around the six years old.

The primary denture is characterized by that the dental arch has a U-shaped and has no compensative curve, the entrainment is unstable because the deciduous teeth are slightly cusped, mandibular teeth are half tooth mesialed from maxillary teeth, anterior teeth are often edge to edge or slight overhang, mesial surfaces of the mandible and maxillary central incisors are aligned with each other and lie on line of the medial sagittal plane. The contact points on temporary teeth are rare, but diastemas are often current. These diastemas aim to ensure a good position for permanent teeth when they erupt.[6]

The posterior occlusion is the relation between the distal surfaces of the second deciduous molars, it is called Chapman plan. It can be straight in most of the cases - 76% of cases, it foreshadows a class I or it can be mesialed -14% of cases, it foreshadows a class I or III or finally distaled -10 % of cases, it foreshadows a class II.

CASE REPORT

A 4-year-old female patient visited the Department of Pediatric and Preventive Dentistry of Padmashree Dr DY Patil Dental College, with the complaint of missing teeth in the maxillary arch and complete absence of teeth in the mandibular arch. She had difficulty in mastication and speech. Peers teased her about her appearance which was constant psychological trauma to the patient and parents. Patient had history of absence of sweating even in hot summer, frequent rise of body temperature since early infancy and getting micturition reflex frequently. Family history revealed consanguineous marriage of parents. Parents and other family members were normal.[7]

On extraoral examination, patient exhibited classical features of ectodermal dysplasia. She had fine sparse hair on scalp and lack of hair on rest of the body, prominent forehead, saddle nose, everted lips.(fig.6)

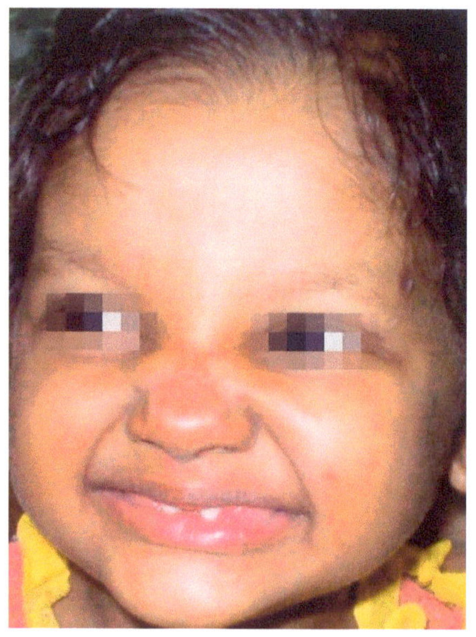

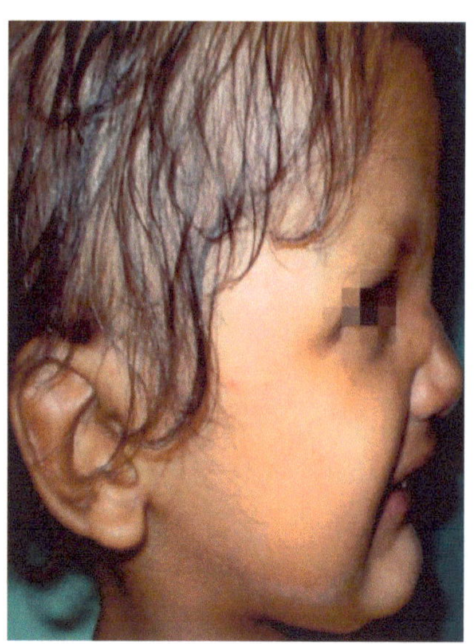

Fig 6

Intraoral examination revealed conical-shaped deciduous centrals, right and left second deciduous molars in the upper arch and edentulous lower arch. She exhibited aplasia of alveolar bone in the edentulous areas.

Radiographic examination: OPG revealed presence of developing permanent canines, right permanent first molar in the upper arch and permanent right first molar in the lower arch.

Removable partial denture for the upper arch and complete denture for the lower arch to restore function, followed by strip crown with composite restoration for conical- shaped deciduous maxillary centrals to give them proper shape and morphology was planned.

Treatment begun with, making upper and lower primary impression with alginate impression material. Specialized custom-made deciduous acrylic trays fabricated on deciduous ideal cast were used for this purpose. Primary casts were prepared. On lower primary cast special tray was fabricated and final impression was obtained with light- body vinyl siloxane impression material. Master cast was obtained from the final impression. Denture base and occlusal rim was constructed. On the upper cast, direct retainer (c clasp) on both deciduous second molars were made, base plate (shellac base plate) was adapted and occlusal rim was constructed.

Jaw relation was recorded. This recorded jaw relation was transferred on to mean value articulator. Teeth arrangement in lower and upper denture base was done. In the next appointment trial dentures were tried for retention, stability, function and esthetic. Lower complete denture and upper removable partial denture was constructed with heat cure acrylic by conventional denture making procedure. Morphological modification of two conical-shaped upper deciduous central incisors with composite strip crowns was done to improve the esthetics. Before delivering the dentures, topical fluoride application was done to maintain the teeth present in the upper arch.

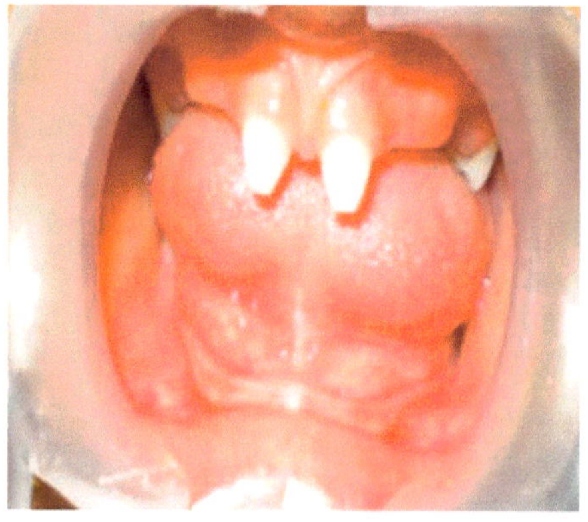

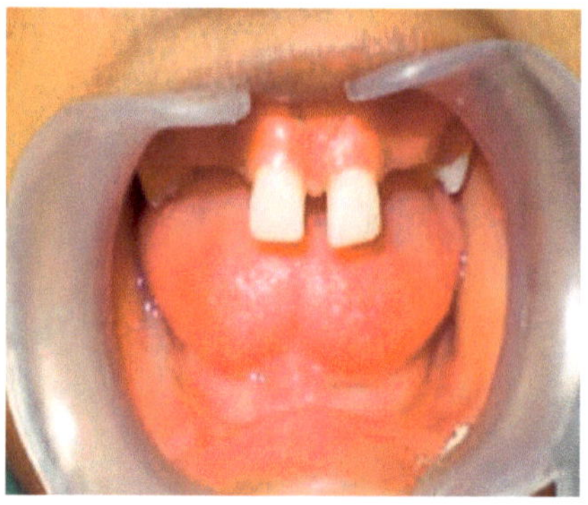

Fig 7

Dentures were delivered. Preoperative and postoperative comparison saw marked improvements in facial form and esthetics. Instructions regarding maintenance of dentures were given and recall appointments were scheduled after 24 hours, 1 and 3 weeks. Fluoride mouthwash was prescribed. After 3 weeks the patient was well adjusted to the dentures. The parents were very happy and stated that there was a significant improvement in her speech and esthetics, and it has contributed toward her psychological well-being. She was scheduled for recall for every 3 months for evaluating her oral hygiene status and maintenance of dentures.

A prosthodontic rehabilitation is fundamental in these situations, attempting to provide a functional and esthetic solution that will allow the child as normal a lifestyle as possible, without damaging self-esteem or psychological development and ensuring that behaviour is unaffected. The prosthetic treatment should be carried out on an individual basis, aimed always toward providing good occlusal stability. Treatment should be commenced as soon as possible in order to avoid possible resorption and atrophy of the alveolar ridges, and to control vertical dimension, which can be severely affected by the total or partial lack of teeth. [7] Removable prosthesis is the most frequently reported treatment modality for the dental management of young ED patients. Because anodontia or hypodontia is typical in individuals with this condition, complete dentures, partial dentures or overdentures are often parts of the treatment provided. Although complete dentures can provide an acceptable esthetic and functional result, underdevelopment of the edentulous alveolar ridges in individuals with ED can compromise denture retention and stability.(fig.7)

Periodic recall of young ED patients is also important because prosthesis modification or replacement will be needed as a result of continuing growth and development. In addition to adjustments related to fit, occlusion of prosthesis must be monitored for ages because of jaw growth.[7]

B-MIXED DENTURE

The mixed denture stage lasts from the age of 6 years with the eruption of the mandibular permanent first molar to the loss of the temporary tooth, usually the maxillary deciduous second molar around the age of 12 years. During this period, the child loses these primary teeth that will be replaced gradually by the permanent teeth.

In mixed dentition there are many chances for early loss of primary tooth as a result of caries, trauma etc, and this premature loss can hinder the arch integrity and the path of eruption of successor tooth, because of the movement of adjacent tooth. So, it is necessary to maintain the tooth space and always the functional harmony of the dentition should be established. Different treatment modalities can be done at this period which indeed can provide a proper equilibrium of maxillary and mandibular tooth. Space maintainers, removable dentures etc can be used based of the tooth that has been exfoliated.

<u>C-PERMANENT DENTURE</u>

Permanent dentures are **an alternative to removable dentures for missing teeth**. Unlike traditional dentures, permanent dentures are typically held in place by two or more surgically-placed dental implants, making them stable and allowing the patient to chew, talk, and smile more easily than with removable dentures.

CHAPTER IV

DECIDUOUS TEETH

Physiological evolution -According to many authors deciduous teeth grow and evolve according to three stages. Fist stage Phase of growth and development, crown and root are build-up. This period lasts about a year. The physiology of dentin-pulp tissue is oriented to repair due to with an important neurovascular bundle and the opening of apex. This process is called dentinogenesis.

Second stage Stage of maturation and stability, which extends from the complete build- up of the root to its clinically detectable resorption. This period lasts three years or less than six months. Dentinogenesis is preserved.

Third stage Regression phase, there is a phenomenon where physiologic root resorption leads to the fall of the deciduous tooth: it is the dental apoptosis. This period lasts three to four Years. Dentinogenesis is compromised. This phase includes structural modifications for the root, the bone and the tissue.[6]

I. FUNCTIONS OF DECIDUOUS TEETH

Deciduous teeth have a crucial aesthetic role as they harmonize the lower floor of the face maintaining occlusion height promoting mandibular growth catch-up. They ensure essential and necessary function for the child for its growth and its physiological, psychological and intellectual development in its environment. These functions include chewing and speaking. Moreover, the temporary teeth promote the evolution of swallowing from a primary state into a mature and physiological state. They are also part of the lower face growth process and occupy a essential role in the development of anterior facial bones .[6]

II. PERIDONTAL TISSUE AROUND DECIDUOUS TEETH

As that of the adult, the child's periodontium is made up of four tissues:

gingival, periodontal ligament, alveolar bone and cementum. However, there are notable differences between the child's periodontal and that of the adult. The gums are often described as being redder, because of more abundant capillary network and thinner epithelium, more translucent, the marginal gingival in stable temporary denture is pink, stiff and elastic, with smooth as peck or finely granite. The cervical anatomy of deciduous teeth and prominence of vestibular wall give it a hemmed thick appearance. The height of the attached gingival is more important in the maxilla than in the mandible and it increases with age. At the diastema, can be observed a gum coated with ortho or para-keratinized sloughing epithelium. The functional epithelium seems less high than the permanent teeth. The width of the periodontal space is increased with of fewer collagen fibers and more important vascularization. The cementum is less dense and thinner, it is acellular in the coronal part of the root and cellular in the apical part.

CHAPTER V

DENTAL TRAUMA AND TYPES

Traumatic injuries not only pose a health risk worldwide, but are also regarded among serious social problems. One important category is dental trauma, accounting for a major part of health problems in children and adolescents. Studies conducted in different countries report various prevalence rates for traumatic dental injuries among children and adolescents. Dental trauma occurs in children mainly because of their weak balance and just having learnt to walk. Demographic evaluations indicate a higher prevalence for trauma in males compared to females. Falling, fight, sports, accidents, and hitting items or people are among common etiologic factors. Home setting, school and street are places with the highest frequency of dental traumatic injuries, which most importantly include enamel fracture and enamel and dentin fracture without pulp exposure.[7]

The trauma can vary from a simple lip laceration to a tooth fracture and even a fracture in the jaw bones. The goal of treatment is to save the teeth.[7]

ETIOLOGY OF TRAUMA TO TEETH

Common etiological factors for traumatic injuries are

- Fall as infant or toddler
- Falls and collisions in school age
- Bicycle and motorcycle injuries
- Contact sports
- Road traffic accidents
- Mental retardation
- Epilepsy
- No accidental injuries (Child abuse)

CHAPTER VI

PREDISPOSING FACTORS FOR DENTAL TRAUMA

- Age of the child—less than 1.5 years—lack of development of neuromuscular coordination.
- Developmental defects of teeth/dental caries—weaken the tooth structure— affecting the resistance to fracture.
- Mental retardation/epilepsy—might result in falls of children—resulting in trauma to the teeth.

Complications of dental injuries to primary teeth.

- Different injuries of teeth involving crown, root or whole tooth
- Failure to continue eruption
- Color changes/discoloration
- Infection and abscess
- Loss of space in the dental arch
- Ankylosis
- Injury to developing permanent teeth
- Abnormal exfoliation
- Financial costs for maintaining dental arch space or restoration

Complications of dental injuries to permanent teeth.
- Color changes
- Infection and abscess
- Loss of space in the dental arch ,Loss of alveolar bone support
- Ankylosis , Resorption of root structure
- Abnormal root development
- Financial costs of potential root canal, restorative, or prosthetic therapy

Various clinical presentations for damage of permanent tooth.

- White/yellow—Brown discoloration of enamel—Turner's tooth
- White/yellow—Brown discoloration of enamel hypoplasia
- Crown dilaceration
- Odontome like malformations
- ■ Root dilaceration
- Vestibular root angulation
- Partial or complete arrest of root formation
- Sequestration of permanent tooth germ
- Disturbance in eruption
- Partial reduplication
- Disturbances in eruption

Types of Dental Trauma to Teeth:

- Subluxation: Mobility of the tooth due to injury to the supporting structures of the tooth.
- Avulsion: tooth is completely displaced out of the tooth socket
  Lateral Luxation: the tooth is displaced and a neighboring bone is fractured.
- Intrusion: the tooth is pushed into the bone
- Extrusion: The tooth is pushed out of the bone
- Fracture of the tooth.

In pediatric dentistry most of the patients are encountered with trauma to the teeth. Based on the extents, types etc many authors have put forward different types of classification to dental trauma.[8]

Classification of anterior teeth trauma by Sweets (1955) [8]

It is mainly based on the anatomy and morphology of the tooth structure. The disadvantages of this classification are that no stress has been laid on injuries to supporting structures soft tissue and bone. It indicates more towards the permanent teeth than primary teeth as injury to periodontium is more common in primary teeth as compared to permanent.

- Class I – A simple of crown exposing no dentition.
- Class II – A parallel of crown involving little dentin.
- Class III – Extensive fracture of crown involving more dentin bur no pulp exposure.
- Class IV – Extensive fracture of crown exposing pulp
- Class V – Complete fracture of crown exposing pulp

- Class VI – Fracture of root with or without loss of crown structure.
- Class VII – Tooth loss as a result of trauma.

Andreasen's Classification of traumatic injuries to teeth.

[7] Injuries to hard dental tissues and pulp

- Class 1: Enamel infraction
- Class 2: Enamel fracture
- Class 3: Enamel—dentin fracture
- Class 4: Complicated crown fracture
- Class 5: Uncomplicated crown—root fracture
- Class 6: Complicated crown—root fracture
- Class 7: Root fracture
- Injuries to periodontal tissues
- Concussion
- Subluxation
- Extrusive luxation
- Intrusive luxation
- Lateral luxation
- Avulsion

Classification by Rabinowitch (1956). [8]

1. Fractures of the enamel or slightly into the dentin
2. Fractures into the dentin
3. Fractures into the pulp
4. Fractures of the periodontium
5. Comminated fractures
6. Displaced teeth.

Benetts Classification (1963) [8]

Benetts classification is according to injuries to periodontium and alveolus considering the anatomy and morphology of the teeth which can be applied partially for primary and permanent teeth.

Class I – Traumatized tooth without coronal or root fracture.
a) Tooth from in alveolus.
b) Tooth subluxated in alveolus.

Class II – Coronal fracture.
a) Involving enamel.
b)Involving enamel + dentin.

Class III – Coronal fracture with pulp exposure.

Class IV – Root fracture
a) Without coronal fracture.
b) With coronal fracture.

Class V – Avulsion of tooth.

This classification tends to simplification. It does not take into account large or small amount of indirect pulp exposure, for from the prevention aspect, the protection of any amount of exposed dentin is equally important.

Crown fractures: -
    a) Of enamel
    b) With indirect pulp exposure through the dentin.
    c) With direct pulp exposure

The shape of the fracture may encompass an angle or more thirds of the crown. The pulp may be clinically normal, hyperaemic, inflamed, or dead. The apical foramina may or may not have completed its physiologic calcification.

Classification by Ellis (1970) [8]

It is a simplified classification, which groups many injuries and allows for subjective interpretation by including broad terms such as simple or extensive or extensive fractures.

Class I - Simple crown fracture with little or no dentin affected

Class II - Extensive crown fracture with considerable loss of dentin, but with the pulp not affected.

Class III - Extensive crown fracture with considerable loss of dentin and pulp exposure.

Class IV - A tooth devitalized by trauma with or without loss of tooth structure.

Class V - Teeth lost as a result of trauma.

Class VI - Root fracture with or without the loss of crown structure.

Class VII - Displacement of the tooth with neither root nor crown fracture

Class VIII - Complete crown fracture and its replacement.

Class IX - Traumatic injuries of primary teeth.

Classification by World Health Organization in its application of International Diseases of Dentistry and Stomatology (1994) [9,10]

This classification is based on a system adopted by the WHO in its application of the international classification of Disease to Dentistry and Stomatology. Certain trauma entities were not defined and included in the WHO system. The following classification includes injuries to the teeth, supporting structures, gingival and oral mucosa and is based on anatomical, therapeutic and prognostic considerations. This classification can be applied to both the primary and the permanent dentition. Includes injuries to the teeth, supporting structure, gingival, and oral mucosa which is based on anatomical, therapeutic and prognostic considerations and applied to both the permanent and the primary dentition. The code number is according to the international classification of diseases to dentistry (1992)

A) Injuries to the hard dental tissues and the pulp [1]

1. Enamel infraction (N 502.50) An incomplete fracture (crack) of the enamel without loss of tooth substance.

2. Enamel fracture (uncomplicated crown fracture) (N 502.50) A fracture with loss of tooth substance confined to the enamel.

3. Enamel- Dentin Fracture (Uncomplicated Crown fracture) (N 502.51) A fracture with loss of tooth substance confined to enamel and dentin, but not involving the pulp.

4. Complicated crown fracture (N 502.52) A fracture involving enamel and dentin, and exposing the pulp.

5. Uncomplicated Crown- Root Fracture (N 502.54) A fracture involving enamel, dentin and cementum, but not exposing the pulp.

6. Complicated Crown-Root fracture (N 502.54) A fracture involving enamel, dentin and cementum, and exposing the pulp.

7. Root Fracture (N 502.53) A fracture involving dentin, cementum, and the pulp. Root fracture can be further classified according to displacement of the coronal fragment, as Horizontal, Oblique, and Vertical.

B) Injuries to the periodontal tissues.

1. Concussion (N 503.20) An injury to the tooth-supporting structures with abnormal loosening on displacement of the tooth, but with marked reaction to percussion.

2. Subluxation (Loosening) (N 503.20) An injury to the tooth-supporting structures with abnormal loosening, but without displacement of the tooth.

3. Extrusive Luxation (Peripheral Dislocation, Peripheral Avulsion) (N 503.20) Partial displacement of the tooth out of its socket.

4. Lateral Luxation (N 503.20) Displacement of the tooth in a direction other than axially. This is accompanied by commutation or fracture of the alveolar socket.

5. Intrusive Luxation (Central dislocation) (N 503.21) Displacement of the tooth into the alveolar bone. This injury is accompanied by commutation or fracture of the alveolar socket.

6. Avulsion (Exarticulation) (N 503.22) Complete displacement of the tooth out of its socket.

C) Injuries to the supporting bone [11]

1. Comminution of the mandibular (N 502.60) or Maxillary (N 502.40) Alveolar Socket Crushing and compression of the alveolar socket. This condition is found concomitantly with intrusive and lateral luxations.
2. Fracture of the Mandibular (N 502.60) or Maxillary (N 502.40) Alveolar Socket Wall A fracture confined to the facial or oral socket wall.
3. Fracture of the Mandibular (N 502.60) or Maxillary (N 502.40) Alveolar process A fracture of the alveolar process which may or may not involve the alveolar socket.

A fracture involving the base of the mandible or maxilla and often the alveolar process (jaw fracture). The fracture may or may not involve the alveolar socket.

Classification of dental trauma of primary teeth by Fried and Erickson (1995) [12]

Classification of hard tissue fractures

- Class I - Simple fracture of enamel only.
- Class II - Fracture involving enamel and dentin.
- Class III - Fracture extends farther into the tooth, with a small pulpal exposure Class IV - Fracture involves significant amount of pulpal exposure
- Class V - Complete loss of the tooth
- Class VI - Fracture of the root

D) Trauma affecting the periodontium

- Concussion - Sensitivity of the tooth to trauma without abnormal loosening or mobility
- Subluxation - Loosening of the tooth without mobility
- Luxation - Displacement of the traumatized teeth.

CHAPTER VII

INFECTIOUS ETIOLOGY

They are mainly represented by tooth decay, but in some situations lead us to extract teeth. In fact, during conditions with bacteraemia risks, it will be necessary to remove infectious sites. Patient with acquired or congenital heart disease, holders of Endo osseous prosthesis or vascular prosthesis as well as children with impaired immune defences present a risk of infection. Dental decay is a post eruptive infectious disease of the hard tissue of the tooth. It is characterized by alternating demineralization and remineralization periods, it is located, from the outside to the inside of the tooth. It affects the hard tissues of the tooth at different degrees, from simple mineral loss, undetectable to the naked eye, to a complete destruction of the tooth. The process is generally reversible in early stages and in favourable conditions, while it is irreversible in advanced stages.

According to the World Health Organization, tooth decay affects approximately five billion people in the world. Decay has consequences in the month, but also at the systemic level, this depends on the overall health of patient, depth and location of the lesion (American academy of pediatric dentistry, 2014).

In children, tooth decay is in the form of rampant caries or baby bottle tooth decay. In the terminal stage, the result of these cavities will lead to multiple extractions. Due to the lesser mineralization and lower thickness of the tissues, carious lesions develop faster in children than in adults

Etiology of decay

Tooth decay is damage that occurs to your teeth, which can potentially result in cavities, dental abscesses, or even tooth loss. It's caused by the activity of certain species of bacteria that can live in dental plaque

The etiology of dental decay is multifactorial. It occurs in the simultaneous action of several factors: the host, the microbial flora, diet and time (Fig.28) and it shows itself only when all these factors are involved. However, it may be inactivated by the absence of one of these factors, in a more contemporary concept it also includes socio-economic aspect as well as psychological and biological factors

Bacteria responsible for decay formation are called cariogenic bacteria. These are mainly bacteria such as Streptococcus, Lactobacillus and Actinomyces. The dietary factor has two components, the sugar content of food on one side and the frequency of food intake on the other side. Other than carbohydrates, no other food component has a cariogenic potential. The sugar considered as cariogenic, the sucrose is considered the most cariogenic, because it is easily metabolized by the cariogenic bacteria, which subsequently will release organic acids resulting in a salivary pH drop which is causing the demineralization process of the tooth. An important factor that is involved in the caries process is the frequency of food intake. In fact, a salivary drop is observed after each feeding.

This risk is shown by Stephan curve

Stages of tooth decay (fig.8)

Stage 1: Initial demineralization

The outer layer of your teeth is composed of a type of tissue called enamel. Enamel is the hardest tissue trusted Source in your body and is mostly made up of minerals. However, as a tooth is exposed to acids produced by plaque bacteria, the enamel begins to lose these minerals. When this occurs, you may see a white spot appear on one of your teeth. This area of mineral loss is an initial sign of tooth decay.

Stage 2: Enamel decay

If the process of tooth decay is allowed to continue, enamel will break down further. You may notice that a white spot on a tooth darkens to a brownish color. As enamel is weakened, small holes in your teeth called cavities, or dental caries, can form. Cavities will need to be filled by your dentist.

Stage 3: Dentin decay

Dentin is the tissue that lies under the enamel. It's softer than enamel, which makes it more sensitive to damage from acid. Because of this, tooth decay proceeds at a faster rate when it reaches the dentin.

Dentin also contains tubes that lead to the nerves of the tooth. Because of this, when dentin is affected by tooth decay, you may begin experiencing sensitivity. You may notice this particularly when having hot or cold foods or drinks.

Stage 4: Pulp damage

The pulp is the innermost layer of your tooth. It contains the nerves and blood vessels that help to keep the tooth healthy. The nerves present in the pulp also provide sensation to the tooth.

When damage to the pulp happens, it may become irritated and start to swell. Because the surrounding tissues in the tooth can't expand to accommodate this swelling, pressure may be placed on the nerves. This can lead to pain

Stage 5: Abscess

As tooth decay advances into the pulp, bacteria can invade and cause an infection. Increased inflammation in the tooth can lead to a pocket of pus forming at the bottom of your tooth, called an abscess. Tooth abscesses can cause severe pain that may radiate into the jaw. Other symptoms that may be present include swelling of the gums, face or jaw,fever, and swollen lymph nodes in your neck.

A tooth abscess requires prompt treatment, as the infection can spread into the bones of your jaw as well as other areas of your head and neck. In some cases, treatment may involve removing the affected tooth.[13]

Stages of Tooth Decay

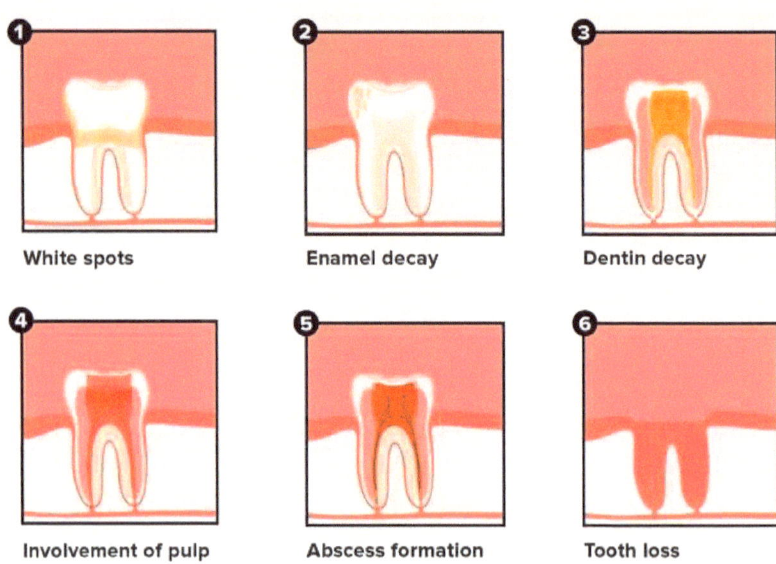

Fig no 8

CHAPTER VIII

CONSEQUENCES OF TOOTH LOSS IN CHILDREN

TOOTH DECAY IN CHILDREN

Children can also experience tooth decay. According to the Centres for Disease Controland Prevention (CDC)Trusted Source, tooth decay is one of the most common chronic childhood conditions in the United States.

Children also may be more likely Trusted Source to experience tooth decay than adults. This is because the enamel of a child's baby teeth is thinner and more sensitive than adult enamel.

Like it does in adults, tooth decay happens when bacteria break down sugars into acids, which damage tooth tissues. Because of this, it's important to make sure your child doesn't consume too much sugary foods or drinks and that their teeth are brushed regularly.

Even though baby teeth are eventually lost, keeping them healthy is still vital. Not only do children need baby teeth for chewing and speaking, they also act as placeholders for adult teeth. If baby teeth are lost too early due to decay, adult teeth may not come in properly.[13]

ARRESTED DECAY

This is due to an interruption of decay process. There is formation of reactive dentin that can be observed clinically and radiologically. The tissues are of hard consistency and dark, there are no symptoms in these lesions. This type of lesion, it can be found on the occlusal surface of the molars and on the proximal surfaces of anterior teeth.(fig.9)

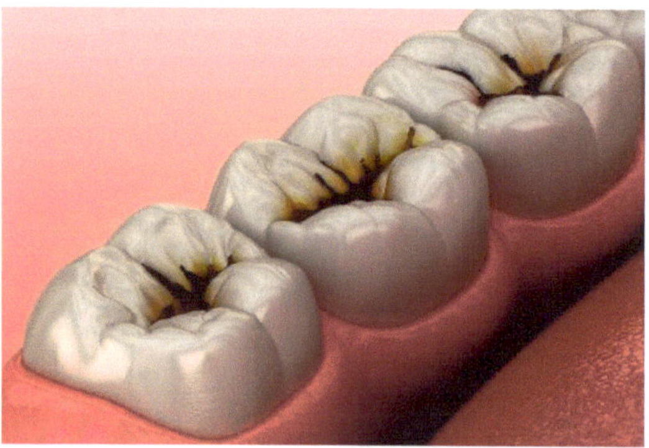

Fig No. 9

Early childhood decay

It is formerly known as rampant caries or baby bottle syndrome. It is characterized by a widespread damage of the teeth with the caries process, it appears very early between two and six years and evolves very quickly (Koch et al., 2009). It is due to the presence of several factors as repeated carbohydrates intake associated with poor hygiene or taking bottle at night before sleep. It is found first on the incisal block of the maxilla, because it is directly exposed to sugar drinks. Decay is rampant or circular and evolutive that can cause crown facture. When the sugar intake or poor eating habits continue, caries appear on the occlusal surfaces of molars (Cameron et al., 2008). The mandibular incisors are less affected by this type of decay, because they are in parts protected by the tongue and salivary flow (Koch et al., 2009).(fig.10)

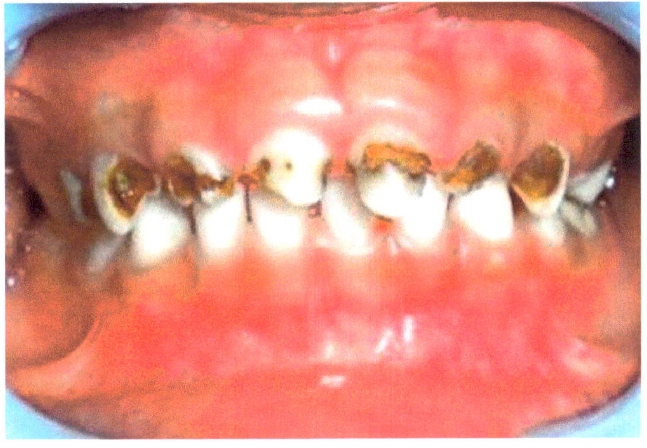

Fig no 10

Congenital etiologies

These etiologies include the anomalies of number, shape, size or structure of the teeth. This may be caused exclusively by a genetic problem, but also the influence of local and systemic factors or combination of all of them. For abnormalities of number of teeth, the terms agenesis or hypodontia are used when the patient has missing teeth due to their non-development. This defect is found mainly in permanent teeth and is rarer in primary dentition. The anodontia described the absence of all the teeth of one or both dental arches. However, the mandible is more affected by the anodontia than the maxilla. The oligodontia is used when there are at least six missing teeth. The abnormalities of tooth form are manifested in many different ways. The dentist can observe conoid teeth, combined, divided the micro and macrodontias. In these cases, the dentist will treat the patient in the permanent dentition because it is few problems in a primary dentition. The structural abnormalities concern attacks that can undergo constituent tissues of the teeth, enamel and dentine. These attacks are hereditary or acquired, they occur during the development of dental organ. In any case these anomalies strengthen the tooth and thus promote the formation of cavities. Some anomalies reach all dental tissues such as regional odontodysplasia. It affects deciduous teeth and corresponding permanent teeth. Anterior teeth and especially maxillary is most often prone to this problem. Other disturbances affect only one tissue either enamel or dentine. When the enamel is produced in small quantities, the result is thinner enamel, this is a hypoplasia. When there is a mineralization defect, this is a hypo mineralisation. In most cases there is a combination of both. When the perturbation reached the dentin, we have the dentinogenesis imperfect, which in clinical is characterized by the opalescent teeth which has brown bluish colour

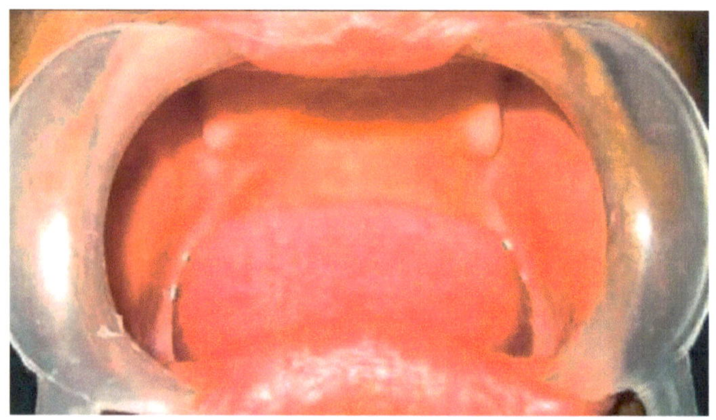

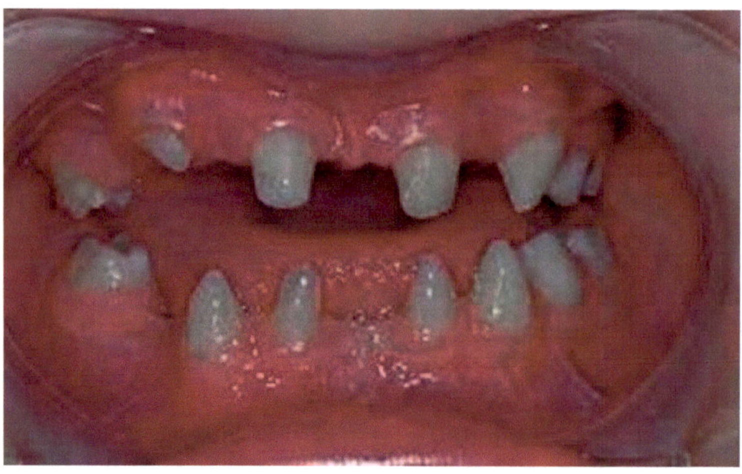

Fig no 11

CONSEQUENCE OF TOOTH LOSS IN CHILDREN

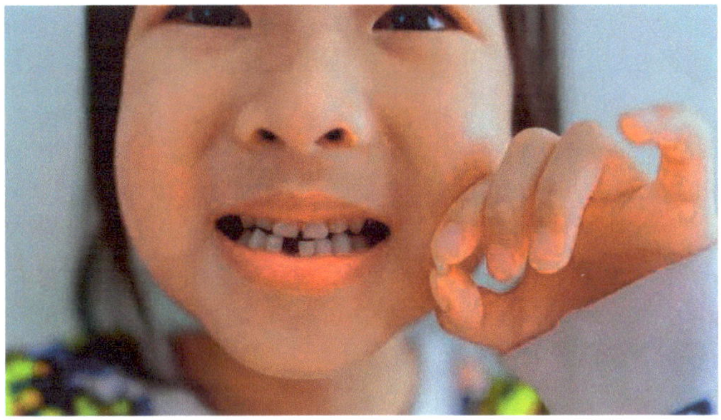

Fig no.12

Tooth loss could result from caries, periodontal disease, trauma, infection, malignancies, or failed endodontic treatments and can present adverse consequences on the remaining dentition and on the patients' general wellbeing. Tooth loss during childhood is very common.(fig.12) It is often regarded as a natural phenomenon because of the exfoliating primary teeth which are eventually replaced by their permanent successors as the child grows. Tooth shedding is a physiological process in the transition of the primary dentition to the permanent and therefore not regarded as tooth loss. However, tooth loss due to various reason is not infrequent in young individuals. Dental injuries and periodontal illness greatly influence the occurrence of tooth loss, but the decay continues to be the main villain of the high rate of loss, males had lost more teeth. Over half of the 1-4 years age group had tooth loss due to trauma, constituting the majority of all the subjects in this category. Hargreaves et al reported trauma to be most common at 4-5 years. Children of 1-4 years age group are toddlers who are very active, adventurous and their feet are not yet stable and are therefore prone to injury from falls and accidents. Overall, the proportion (10.8%) of subjects who lost their teeth prematurely due to trauma in our study is comparable with the reports of other studies. Tooth loss either by extraction or due to trauma can be very distressing in the young child. The horrifying experience, associated pain and sight of blood in both instances can have a long-lasting negative impact on the child. Tooth loss for orthodontic reasons and eruption disorders surpassed that of trauma, a finding that is similar to reports by Folayan et al. [16] This trend is probably an indication of an increased awareness on dental aesthetics and appearance in the populace. Tooth loss due to failure of previous treatment such as pulp therapy may be inevitable in certain situations when children present late for treatment. However, careful selection and diagnosis with adequate clinical skills is paramount to minimize treatment failure. Tooth loss due to periodontal diseases and infections was not represented in our study, confirming the assertion of Folayan et al,[16] that periodontal disease as a cause of tooth extraction in children is on the decline. Premature loss of primary teeth and loss of permanent teeth during childhood frequently results in compromised aesthetics and function, drifting and tipping of adjacent teeth, leading to crowding and impaction of permanent successors and other types of malocclusions. Premature loss of primary molars in particular frequently result in arch space loss as the child grows. Space loss can also arise when the primary 1st molar is lost before or during active eruption of the 1 permanent molar. More primary teeth were lost in this study and most of the tooth loss were seen in the mandible in both dentitions. This is similar to in a way the primary second molar was more frequently lost than the primary first molar This observation is a pointer to the appropriate use of space maintainers to prevent arch space loss in the growing child in our community. More teeth were lost in the mandibular arch when compared with the maxillary arch in both dentitions. The greater loss of teeth in the mandibular arch might be due to food packing potential and greater plaque accumulation in the mandibular posterior region in contrast to the relative abundance of saliva and its anti-carious effect to maxillary molar teeth. [14] Although the maxillary central incisor was the most frequently lost anterior tooth in both dentitions, the most frequently lost permanent tooth was the mandibular first molar as reported in many other studies. The mandibular first permanent molar is the most caries prone tooth in the permanent dentition probably as a result of its long exposure to the oral environment. It is pertinent to prevail on parents and care givers to institute measures that will protect children and adolescents from unwarranted tooth loss. It is important to enhance the oral health awareness of children and adolescents by conducting school dental health programs. Parents and their children should be made to realize the deleterious effect of early loss of teeth and the importance of the primary teeth. All efforts should be made to preserve them. Early presentation at the clinic will forestall unwarranted tooth extractions. The parents of those children should be advised to bring their children to the dental hospital for the procedures to be done.

41

CHAPTER IX

PROSTHETIC REHABILITATION IN THE CHILDREN

Prosthodontic rehabilitation is possible and necessary in childhood as in adulthood, mostly in cases of premature tooth loss. Every tooth loss before it's a physiological shift, and/or congenital absence of teeth may cause dysfunctions of the orofacial system, carrying several other complications from the functional, aesthetic and psychological point of view.[17]

The prosthetic treatment is frequent in adults, however, in some case it is necessary to realize removable or fixed prosthesis on children. Before any proposal, assessment of risk-benefit ratio of treatment is studied, if it is beneficial, care will be continued. The objectives of prosthetic treatment in children are to restore aesthetics, maintain the space and the length of the arches as well as the vertical dimension, maintain or regain functions and prevent the occurrence of parafunction

Premature teeth loss, both deciduous and permanent, may cause functional problems in children, such as malfunctions in mastication, improper teeth placement or eruption and hindered pronunciation. Esthetical issues are also present, as child may be mocked or bullied, leading to insecurity, development of complexes and low self-esteem.

Modern dental prosthetic appliances need to fulfil several important criteria in order to be considered as an adequate treatment option in children:[18]

1. Rehabilitation of masticatory functions and efficiency: Prosthetic appliance needs to be able to replace missing teeth without hindering child's ability to chew. They must be designed properly to avoid or minimize wear on the opposing dentition.
2. Protection of dental pulp: Vitality of dental pulp should be preserved whenever possible. Prosthetic restoration must be made with great care not to disturb vitality of the tooth it is on (if vital), as well as adjacent or opposite teeth. Prosthetic restoration needs to be regularly checked and

adjusted accounting for child's growth and development.

3. Esthetic criteria: Restoring esthetics is one of the pillars of modern dentistry. Caring about personal appearance is very important to children, especially in adolescence1. However, there are recent studies showing that even children in preschool period (age 3-5) have a developed consciousness about their body image, and do care about how they are perceived by other children and adults alike.

4. Proper speech function: Missing teeth, especially in anterior regions, may cause improper speech. Missing incisors often lead to a child being unable to properly pronounce dental consonants such as "t", "d", "n" and in some language's "l". Similar problems may develop in children with cheilo-gnato-palatoschisis. This may lead to development of improper speech patterns that need to be corrected with the aid of speech therapist after the missing teeth or defects are taken care of with adequate prosthetic appliance.

5. Prosthetic appliance must support optimal and proper development of teeth and their eruption, as well as support growth of the dental arches, and facial bones. Prosthetic appliances need to be regularly maintained, adjusted and checked in order to prevent them from inhibiting proper orofacial development. In that sense, considering the fluid and changing environment of a child's oral cavity, all dental prosthetic appliances have a temporary function.

6. Prevention of harmful habits: missing teeth or improper teeth alignment may cause the child to develop bruxism (teeth grinding), or to repeatedly clench their jaws. These habits can also develop in some children as a response to pain, sometimes during teeth eruption. Also, kids with certain medical condition, such as cerebral palsy, are also prone to develop bruxism. The purpose of the adequate prosthetic appliance in these cases is to prevent harmful habit by stabilizing occlusion and preventing painful sensations.

7. Provision of space maintenance: If the missing teeth are not replaced with a prosthetic appliance, adjacent teeth can migrate towards the toothless alveolar ridge, leading to occlusion problems and issues with dental eruption.

Fixation of loosened teeth after trauma: Splints, both wire and composite or fibres, perform a crucial role in saving teeth that have been loosened by trauma. Detailed examination with x-rays must be performed before splinting the teeth, and regular dentist supervision and check-ups must be maintained for the duration of the splint, to avoid ankylosis.

All of these criteria must be fulfilled in order to create appropriate conditions for definite prosthodontics once the adult age is reached.

In the past, when deciduous tooth was suffering from extensive decay, most often outcome for such tooth was extraction. Pulpotomy treatment, and large carious lesions on primary teeth often led to failure of direct restorations, due to inability provide adequate, saliva free working environment and sufficient retention.

Nowadays, crowns are considered a viable alternative. Indications for use of dental crowns on deciduous teeth are:[19]

1. Developmental defects
2. Fractured teeth
3. Teeth after pulpal therapy
4. Restoring multisurface caries, especially in patients with high caries risk
5. Teeth with extensive wear
6. Teeth that need to function as an abutment for space maintainer.

CHAPTER X

REMOVABLE DENTURE FOR A CHILD

Removable denture has the characteristic of being removed and installed by the patient. Partial dentures are made of a resin base plate (in general polymethyl methacrylate), shaped steel clasps and artificial teeth in resin. Complete dentures do not include clasps. Orthodontic devices may be integrated at the prosthesis to support or stimulate the growth phenomenon. They may also be used to correct occlusion defects or dental positioning.[20]

I. DESCRIPTION

Young children with hypodontia caused by ectodermal dysplasia not only have difficulties in mastication and speech but can also sense that their appearance is different from others. Enabling children with ED to look like their peers through the use of well-fitting and functioning complete and removable partial dentures with age- appropriate teeth will greatly assist in their transitioning in to their school years and add to their psychological well-being. Although denture construction requires multiple patient appointments and good co-operation, dentist also should educate and encourage parents and patient to tackle the difficulties that may come across during denture construction.

Partial removable dentures in children must be planned with child growth and development in mind. Design of dentures must be such that it allows for modification when teeth erupt or migrate. That said, long periods without a tooth (or tooth replacement) lead to narrowing of alveolar processes and vertical alveolar defects at sites with missing teeth, over eruption of unopposed permanent teeth, and tipping of adjacent teeth 12.

A-Tissue supported partial dentures are indicated when we expect a child to be without a tooth for a prolonged period of time, or when bone resorption and remodelling is anticipated immediately following extraction or traumatic tooth loss.

They are also indicated in severe cases of hypodontia, weather hereditary (like ectodermal dysplasia) or after cyst or tumour operations. Denture fabrications in early age, especially in cases of hypodontia, may lead to significant improvements in appearance, speech and masticatory functions. Such positive changes may increase the self-confidence of the child and aid in establishing proper dietary patterns. Balla et al. showed that wearing tissue supported dentures does not inhibit maxillary or mandibular growth [21]

Retention of tissue supported dentures in children is most often achieved by extended body of acrylic base of the denture, resting on alveolar ridge and palate. Clasps are only used, when necessary, due to force they administer to teeth, but some orthodontic springs may be incorporated in the design of the denture to facilitate necessary tooth movement (if needed). In recent years, polyamide-based dentures have started to be more frequently used in paediatric dentistry, mainly due to its higher elasticity, toxicological safety and good esthetic14. Their high adaptability and elasticity make them especially suited for use in deciduous and mixed dentition period.

B-Teeth supported dentures can be designed in edentulous states following cyst or tumour operations in mandibular or maxillary region.

In these cases, it would not be advisable to apply pressure on compromised gingival or bone tissues, as that could lead to post-operative complications, ulcerations and infections. Retention of teeth supported dentures is achieved via dental clasps and occlusal rests, minimizing as much as possible contact with mucosae, while rigidity of the denture is ensured by the supportive metal frame.

All dentures designed must allow for proper hygienic maintenance of both denture and child's oral cavity, and ensure no damage to surrounding tissues. Regular check-ups and recalls must be made every 3-6 months, and modifications must be made to match and accommodate to child's growth and development. Loss of anterior teeth in children and adolescents is more often a result of injury and/or complication from previous trauma (like ankylosis or root resorption). Central maxillary incisors are teeth most frequently affected by trauma. During period of childhood, and especially in puberty, a non-invasive long term interim restoration should be designed until implant is indicated. Because of risk of complications such as implant infraposition, implant therapy should be postponed until adulthood is reached.[21]

C-Resin bonded or resin retained bridges represent a minimally invasive option for replacing missing teeth. This type of restoration was first described in 1970's, and since then, they have evolved significantly in both design and materials used. First type of resin bonded bridge was known as Rochettebridge, which generated its retention through resin cement bonding through characteristic perforated metal retainer. The commonly used nickname for resin retained bridges "Maryland bridge" results from the type of electrochemical etching developed at university of Maryland, which improved and enhanced resin bonding to the metal alloy. In recent years, with development of new materials, traditional metal-resin restorations are starting to slowly be abandoned in favour of modern fibre reinforced composites. Evolution of fibre products for dental use has transitioned from plain fibres, over pre-impregnated fibres to fully resin impregnated fibres. Most common types of fibres for use in resin bonded bridges are polyethylene, Kevlar and glass-based fibres. Also, the fibres may be unidirectional, braid, mesh/network or woven. Different types of fibres and weaves create different adaptability and manageability, as well as different capabilities to distribute the force multidirectional. Majority of clinical studies of resin bonded bridges report on unidirectional fibres, and out of those, most used are glass fibres, mainly due to their strength and aesthetics. The use of fibre reinforced composites in resin bonded restorations is advised for their favourable elastic module in comparison to metal, and better adhesion of the composite to the framework. Main advantages of resin bonded bridges are their preservance of healthy tooth substance, needing no or minimal preparations, reduced costs and generally good patient acceptance. Also, they tend to remove pressure from mucosae and alveolar ridge (unlike tissue supported partial denture), therefore reducing the risk of alveolar bone resorption and possible complications with future implant therapy. Careful planning is needed in order properly distribute masticatory pressure on the adjacent teeth. Resin bonded bridges are relatively easy also.

Most common reasons of failure of resin bonded bridge are de-bonding, and discoloration and chipping, especially in areas where fibres have been exposed to oral cavity. Majority of the studies show that the expected survival rate of resin bonded bridge to be around 72-74% after the period of 3-5 years. Also, it is reported that anterior restorations can be expected to last longer than posterior ones, as well as that survival rate of resin bonded bridges in maxilla is higher as opposed to mandible (81% vs 56% after 2.5 years). There is however a definite lack of detailed, standardized information in the literature concerning longevity of resin bonded bridges.

The removable partial denture has the following components: denture base, clasps and the artificial teeth.[22]

The Denture Base

It corresponds to the support of various prosthetic elements; it is made of polymethyl methacrylate. It ensures the stability and sustenance of the prosthetic assembly. These prostheses have the particularity to present osteo- mucous support, for that the surface must be maximized and the edges avoid prevent insertion of the muscles so as not cause disinsertion of the prosthesis during various movements [23]

The posterior limit is determined by the evolution of the first permanent molars. If their eruption is close - within 6months – the posterior limit must stop distally of the second deciduous molar, if their eruption is late, the maxillary tuberosity and the retromolar pad are covered [24].

In complete denture, stabilization and retention are more difficult to obtain due to the lack of teeth and the lack of bony embosses due to the resorption.[25]

Clasps (fig.13)

Clasps are metal components which emerge out from denture and encircle the tooth. They come in various designs and are placed into undercut areas to provide an adequate fixation and retention.[25] Some commonly used clasps are Adam's clasp, circumferential clasp and ball end clasp. Adam's clasp can be used even in partially erupted molars. They provide the majority of retention, they come on the mesial and distal embrasures of the molars. They are easily modifiable. The circumferential clasp is used at the canine level and sometimes can be placed on the permanent molars. They will look retention in the buccal undercuts and this retention can be completed by adding ball end clasp positioned between canine and first deciduous molar [25,26]

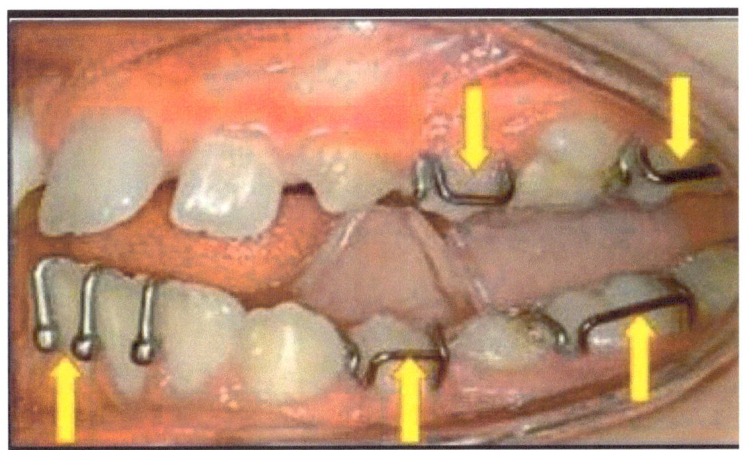

<u>Artificial teeth(fig.14)</u>

For children, there are resin teeth, but the selection of teeth and colours is very limited. These teeth meet the requirements of occlusal child's arch as the absence of compensation curve. In some cases, it would be possible to use small size adult teeth but it is not advised because they do not have the same characteristics.[27]

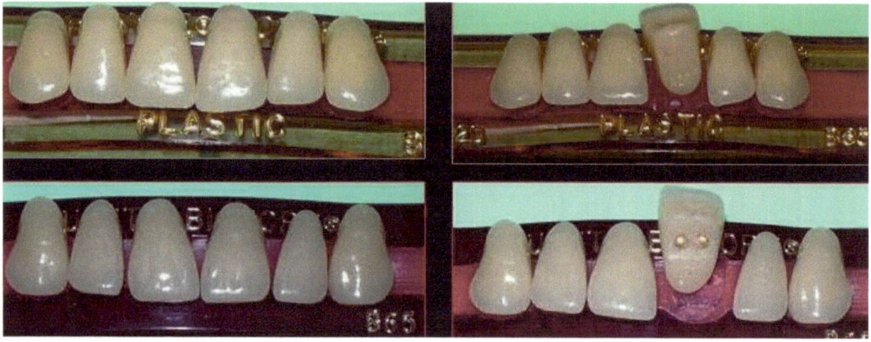

Fig no 14

II. INDICATION

Removable dentures are indicated to replace several teeth in the same quadrant or in both quadrants of the same arch, also in case of premature loss of primary teeth and when restoration of masticatory function is important and finally in case of congenital absence of teeth. The removable denture can also serve as space maintainer. It should be noted, the ideal requirements of removable dentures. The denture should restore the lost aesthetics, it should improve masticatory function, not interfere with the normal growth of dental arches. It should be easy for the child to use, cleaned easily and should allow adjustments, if necessary.[27]

III. COMPLETE AND REMOVABLE PARTIAL PROSTHESIS FOR A CHILD WITH HYPOHIDROTIC ECTODERMAL DYSPLASIA [A CASE REPORT] [28]

A 4-year-old female patient visited the Department of Pediatric and Preventive Dentistry of Padmashree Dr DY Patil Dental College, with the complaint of missing teeth in the maxillary arch and complete absence of teeth in the mandibular arch. She had difficulty in mastication and speech. Peers teased her about her appearance which was constant psychological trauma to the patient and parents.(fig.16)

Patient had history of absence of sweating even in hot summer, frequent rise of body temperature since early infancy and getting micturition reflex frequently. Family history revealed consanguineous marriage of parents. Parents and other family members were normal.

On extraoral examination, patient exhibited classical features of ectodermal dysplasia. She had fine sparse hair on scalp and lack of hair on rest of the body, prominent forehead, saddle nose, everted lips.

Intraoral examination revealed conical-shaped deciduous centrals, right and left second deciduous molars in the upper arch and edentulous lower arch. She exhibited aplasia of alveolar bone in the edentulous areas.

Radiographic examination: OPG revealed presence of developing permanent canines, right permanent first molar in the upper arch and permanent right first molar in the lower arch.(fig.15)

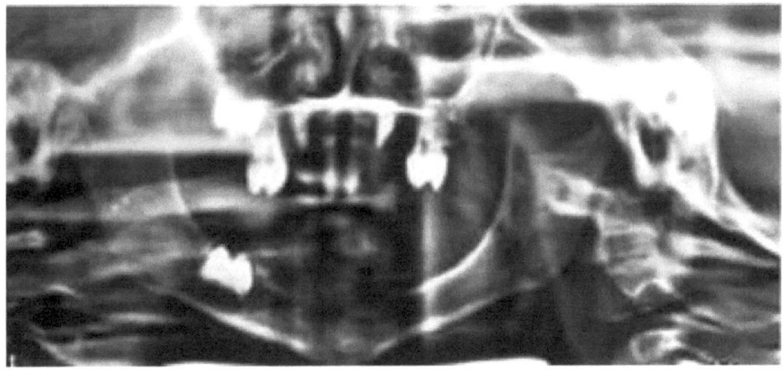

Fig no 15

Treatment- begun with, making upper and lower primary impression with alginate impression material. Specialized custom-made deciduous acrylic trays fabricated on deciduous ideal cast were used for this purpose. Primary casts were prepared.

On lower primary cast special tray was fabricated and final impression was obtained with light-body vinyl siloxane impression material. Master cast was obtained from the final impression. Denture base and occlusal rim was constructed. On the upper cast, direct retainer (c clasp) on both deciduous second molars were made, base plate (shellac base plate) was adapted and occlusal rim was constructed. Jaw relation was recorded.

This recorded jaw relation was transferred on to mean value articulator. Teeth arrangement in lower and upper denture base was done. In the next appointment trial dentures were tried for retention, stability, function and aesthetic

Lower complete denture and upper removable partial denture was constructed with heat cure acrylic by conventional denture making procedure. Morphological modification of two conical-shaped upper deciduous central incisors with composite strip crowns was done to improve the aesthetics

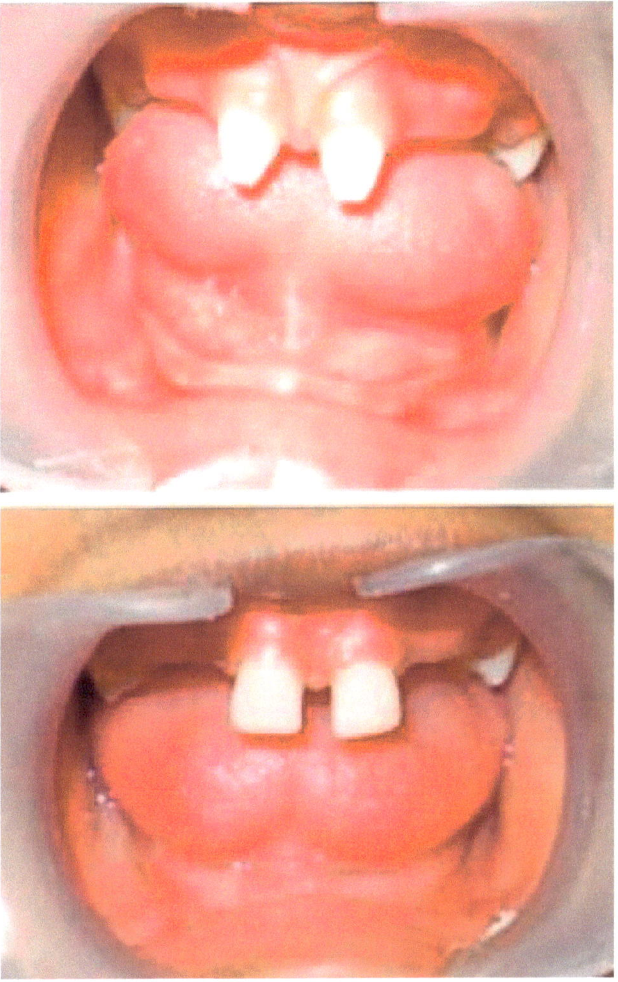

Fig no 16

Before delivering the dentures, topical fluoride application was done to maintain the teeth present in the upper arch. Dentures were delivered. Preoperative and postoperative comparison saw marked improvements in facial form and aesthetics [Fig. 50]. Instructions regarding maintenance of dentures were given and recall appointments were scheduled after 24 hours, 1 and 3 weeks. Fluoride mouthwash was prescribed. After 3 weeks the patient was well adjusted to the dentures. The parents were very happy and stated that there was a significant improvement in her speech and aesthetics, and it has contributed toward her psychological well-being. She was scheduled for recall for every 3 months for evaluating her oral hygiene status and maintenance of dentures.

A prosthodontic rehabilitation is fundamental in these situations, attempting to provide a functional and aesthetic solution that will allow the child as normal a lifestyle as possible, without damaging self-esteem or psychological development and ensuring that behaviour is unaffected. The prosthetic treatment should be carried out on an individual basis, aimed always toward providing good occlusal stability. Treatment should be commenced as soon as possible in order to avoid possible resorption and atrophy of the alveolar ridges, and to control vertical dimension, which can be severely affected by the total or partial lack of teeth. When the patient growth is completed and a more stable and fixed situation is established, possibility of provisional fixed prostheses and of implant treatment can be considered.

IV. PATIENT MONITORING

After the final insertion, the patient and parents are instructed in routine oral hygiene for maintenance of dentures and recall appointments is scheduled after two days and once in the following weeks to see the difficulties encountered by the patient or make some adjustments to the denture if necessary. Post instruction should be instructed to the patients and has to be followed mandatory for better oral health and more hygienic shelf life.[29]

Partial dentures only work well if they are kept in good condition, which is an easy thing to do. Clean the partial dentures at least twice a day, take care not to drop the dentures, never wear the dentures to sleep, Soak the dentures overnight, do not hesitate to go to the dentist.[30]

CHAPTER XI

THE FIXED PROSTHESIS IN CHILDREN

Unlike removable denture, this type of prosthesis is fixed, it is placed by the dentist and the patient cannot remove.

i. Indications and contraindications to the fixed prosthesis

As for removable dentures, cooperation of the child and parents is critical to the longevity of the treatment as well as the oral dental hygiene. Fixed prosthesis is indicated on deciduous teeth that need to remain more than two years in the arch, when extensive carious lesions undermine cusps and expand beyond line angles. This prosthesis is also indicated following pulpotomy or pulpectomy or to replace failure of other available restorative materials [31]. However, when the damage from caries is just occlusal with no proximal involvements, conservative restorations as composite or amalgams is indicated. Fixed prosthesis is contraindicated when the tooth exhibits mobility, when there is clinical and/or radiographic evidence of radicular pathology [31]

ii. Different types of fixed prosthesis

Dentist now a days, uses different types of pediatric crowns: stainless steel, composite strip, polycarbonate, resin-veneered and zircon ceramic. Each of these crown types has advantages and disadvantages that dictate its suitability for different applications. Some of the most important factors considered by dentists when choosing a crown type are durability, aesthetics, retentiveness adaptability, placement time, allergenicity, and cost.

Dental crowns are prosthetics which are used to cover up misshapen teeth and restore the smile on your face. We've seen a number of villains smile wide with stainless steel crowns. If your teeth are weak or broken, these crowns are an excellent fix. They are also used to provide support in case you are getting a dental bridge.

Pediatric Dental Crowns for Child's Baby Teeth

Dental Crowns are a marvel of medical innovation that has solved many complex dentistry problems in the modern day. A dental crown can be an easy alternative to many problems that used to require interventive treatment such as root canal or tooth; extraction. Many of these treatments cannot be performed on patients with age and medical limitations. Therefore, there was a need for an easier solution for a tooth that was damaged and needed replacement.

Pediatric Crowns is a sub-branch under dental crowns that is especially designed for children's baby teeth. Children with baby teeth cannot have extensive dental treatments nor are they capable of undergoing many of the surgical treatment forms. This is why there was a need for alternative options that did not cause any adverse reactions in kids and remained safe post installation as well.

Dental and Pediatric Crowns

Dental Crowns are caps that are placed strategically on top of the broken or damaged tooth. They are made from many different kinds of materials and can help in solving many purposes. A dental crown is recommended in many scenarios such as:

- When a tooth has become weak due to damage or infection

- When a tooth has cracked

- For restoration of a broken tooth

- To fit onto a worn-down tooth

- Covering tooth that has a large filling

- Covering a dental Implant or a Bridge

- To cover a misshapen tooth or a discoloured tooth

- Covering tooth that has been worn down after Root Canal Treatment

Getting a dental crown is one of the most common dental procedures these days as their usage is very flexible and versatile and solves many purposes with just a single option. It also comes in many different forms of material and can be chosen based on the type of teeth, the position of the teeth and the preference of the patient.

Pediatric Crowns or Pediatric Dental Crowns are made specifically for baby teeth. They are a different division under dental crowns as they are made from sensitive and non- allergic materials that are used to help children maintain their dental functions while their permanent teeth grow in place. They are also one of the safest options for kids who need medical intervention.

Although baby teeth do not last many years, an untreated teeth can bring in more problems in the future and create a bad foundation for permanent teeth that grow in later. Below are some of the main reasons children's baby teeth can need replacement with pediatric crowns:

- Baby teeth that has bacterial and gum infection

- Teeth that has become weak or soft because of decay

- Teeth that has chipped

- Teeth that is misshapen

- Teeth that is discoloured

- Teeth that is broken or fractured due to accidents

These are some of the top cases where a child may require pediatric dental crowns as an alternative for their primary teeth. One of the biggest reasons why pediatric crown is required is because primary teeth cannot be left untreated even for small and minor issues. An untreated problem can lead to the growth of unhealthy secondary or permanent teeth. If the shape of the teeth is not preserved, the permanent teeth growing in may be misshapen and out of order. It may then require orthodontic procedures for corrections later on.

Most parents tend to leave small tooth infections or deformity unattended, thinking that they would soon fall out and would be taken over by permanent teeth, but the fact is, the foundation of the tooth is bad, there is a high chance that the teeth that grow in that place will also be similar.

Another reason why children need to preserve their primary teeth is because at their age, it is important for them to learn proper skills that depend on healthy teeth such as speech, enunciation and chewing ability. All of these factors can be affected if they do not have a good set of primary teeth.

These are some of the reasons why primary teeth must be taken good care of and in case of any dental deformity, they must be preserved and corrected with the use of dental procedures and solutions.

I. Stainless Steel Crowns

Stainless steel crowns are extra-coronal restorations that are used particularly in the restoration of grossly broken-down teeth and large multi-surface cavities. The placement of traditional stainless-steel crowns can be challenging for the patient as well as the clinician since it is associated with tooth preparation.[32]

Stainless steel crowns, also referred to as preformed metal crowns were introduced by Humphrey to pediatric dentistry in 1950. They are used as an alternative to silver and tooth-colored fillings. Most of them last four years or more and they also have a polished surface that makes it easy to cleanse. They are also known as silver crowns and are employed in the case of badly broken primary teeth or milk teeth. They are durable, corrosion-resistant, inexpensive, and help in safeguarding the decayed teeth of children.

Stainless steel crowns are used to repair a decayed molar by professional dentists. It also prevents the teeth from further decaying. They are made in the exact size of a child's molar. They are subjected to negligible sensitivity during replacement and offer the advantage of full coronal coverage. It is possible to place a well-fitting crown without compromising the quality or longevity of a crying child. Therefore, stainless steel crowns are used in restoration due to an inability to control the secretion of saliva.[32]

SOME FACTS ABOUT STAINLESS STEEL CROWNS

- Contains only safe metals
- Does not impair the growth of permanent teeth
- Are easy and simple to apply
- Will fall out naturally when the child's teeth fall out
- Offers an alternative in removing a decayed tooth
- Stainless steel dental crowns are used by dentists and orthodontists throughout the globe.
- Stainless steel crowns are used mostly as a temporary fix while some other crown made from another material is being processed.
- These dental crowns are made only out of metals that are safe and will not cause irritation.
- Stainless steel crowns are used on children in order to fit a primary tooth that has been made to fit it.
- You can get a stainless-steel crown installed in a single visit to the dentist.
- Stainless steel dental crowns are less expensive than other dental crowns.

CHAPTER XII

STAINLESS STEEL CROWNS FOR ADULTS

Stainless steel dental crowns are preformed metal crowns that can be used on teeth. They are used primarily on milk teeth, mostly in the back. They are not preferred on front milk teeth because they are distinct and not very flattering.(fig.17)

What most people do not know is that stainless steel crowns are also used on permanent molars in adults.

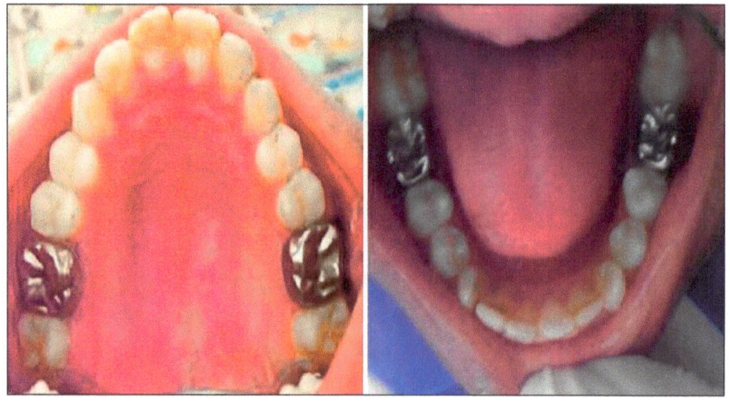

Fig no 17

STAINLESS STEEL CROWNS FOR CHILDREN

Since they were invented in the 1950s, these stainless-steel crowns have been very effective on milk teeth. As they are preformed, they sit well on teeth and perform all the basic functions that the crown of a tooth would.(fig.18)

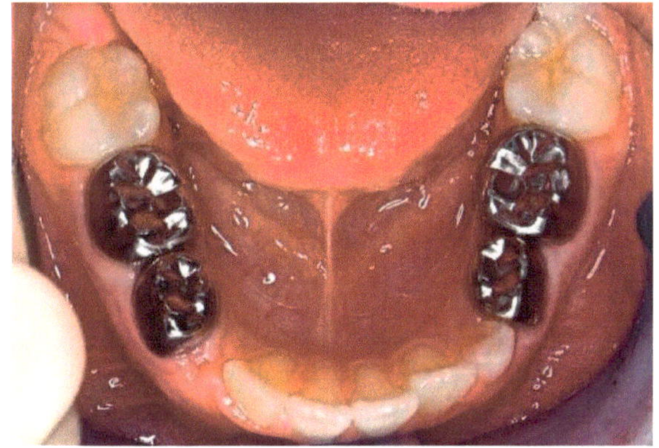

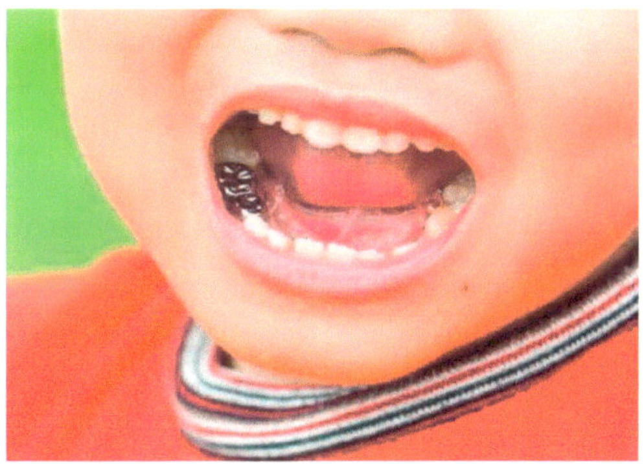

Fig no 18

It is also extremely convenient that the stainless-steel crown will fall off easily when the milk tooth does, without causing any complications. Furthermore, this dental crown is built to last long until the tooth actually falls out. You need not pay many visits to the dentist until then.

Stainless Steel Crowns (or SSCs) are preformed metal crowns that help in protecting baby (primary) teeth. As the name implies, they are metal crowns, which are made of stainless steel and contain chrome & nickel. [33]

If your child is physically or mentally disabled and cannot be subjected to intensive oral care and maintenance, stainless steel crowns are the best option for them. These dental crowns can also be used to repair damaged and broken teeth.[33]

When a tooth is severely damaged due to dental caries or needs to undergo pulp treatment, a stainless-steel crown is the best option. Any abnormal birth defects on your teeth can also be combated with the use of a stainless-steel dental crown.

Please keep in mind to consult your dentist before picking out the dental crown that will work for you. If you are allergic to metal, this dental crown is not for you.

These prefabricated crowns are adapted to the damaged teeth and cemented with biocompatible luting agents. They are popular in fixing a lost tooth, helping to improve the overall structure of the young teeth.

They were introduced by Dr William Humphrey & Engel in 1950 as chrome-steel. Later, in the 1960s, they were significantly improved by Unitek. Since then, a lot of studies have been conducted and as a result, SSCs have been proven superior when compared to an amalgam restoration, especially for multi-surface cavities in primary molars. [33]

Benefits of Using Stainless Steel Crowns

Dentists offer different types of dental crowns like the ones made from zirconium oxide & resin. Though these options are readily available, the classic remains as such. When you compare stainless steel crowns with other restorative materials, their success rate is about 96%. Besides this, the benefits of stainless-steel crowns are diverse, which include:

- **Affordability**: When compared to others, stainless steel crowns are less expensive and tend to have more perks than them.

- **Durability**: According to research, steel caps are highly helpful in keeping even the badly damaged teeth in shape. It is one of the best alternatives to any other non-durable, aesthetic option such as ceramic, porcelain or white zirconia dental crowns. Stainless Steel Crowns are perfect for posterior teeth.

- **Adaptability**: Generally, dentists do not prefer using SSCs for adults. But they could assist in conditions where a patient suffers from a health issue and all the other options are difficult. This sounds ideal during situations like pregnancy and senior citizens.
- **Ease of Use:** Most dental crowns require attaching them to the damaged tooth without bleeding or moisture getting in the way. But SSCs do not have sensitivity to such factors. A dentist can smoothly contour and trim the steel caps for that "perfect" fit.
- **Increases Strength:** The main goal of using a stainless steel crown is to help restore a tooth's size & shape, enhance its strength, and make it look much better. Therefore, for patients, who really need them, they make a huge difference for their oral hygiene. They are also perfect for teeth that are involved in breaking down food, chewing and grinding, therefore taking upon a considerable amount of labour.[34]
- **Complete Coverage**: A stainless steel crown is a wonderful alternative to tooth- colored and silver fillings. Since it is a durable metal cap, it offers complete coverage to the damaged tooth. In most cases, where the posterior or back teeth are damaged, tooth-colored alternatives may not be suitable as they cannot cover the entire space and shape of the teeth. This is where the Stainless-Steel crown comes into picture.

Easy Maintenance: SSCs have a polished and smooth surface. This feature makes them completely easy to maintain and clean. When well-maintained, they can last for 4 years or even more. They are also quite cheaper when compared to tooth coloured alternatives and require much less upkeep. The maintenance is quite easy and it hardly ever requires a re-visit to the dentist for re- examination. [34]

When are Stainless Steel Crowns Used?

A dentist suggests stainless steel crowns for children during any one of the following:

- Restore a broken or severely damaged tooth
- Protect a weak tooth
- Cover a dental implant
- Hold a dental bridge in place

- Recurring dental caries
- Rampant dental caries
- Extensive decalcification
- Extensive dental caries
- After a pulp therapy
- Severe bruxism (or tooth grinding)
- Acquired or inherited enamel defects
- Kids with higher rate of dental cariesFractured or broken tooth
- Abnormal tooth structure from the birth
- Abnormal tooth structure due to a disease
- For intermediate restoration [35]

When are Stainless Steel Crowns Not Used?

A stainless-steel crown is never suggested in any of these cases:

- Individuals with nickel allergy
- Teeth that cannot be restored
- Mobile teeth
- Molars with half of the roots or more are resorbed
- Primary molars that are next to exfoliation The potential risks of using SSCs include:
- Unaesthetic or looks unpleasing
- Cannot be used if the patient is allergic to nickel
- Substantial amount of tooth structure is discarded
- Gingival inflammation because there is unremoved excess cement [35]

TYPES OF STAINLESS-STEEL CROWNS FOR CHILDREN

Stainless steel crowns that were used earlier posed issues in technique due to poor anatomy and gingival contours. However, the crowns that are used today, have lesser problems due to their festooned gingival contours, wide range of sizes, and shallow cuspal anatomy. When it comes to pediatric dentistry, the most common options used today are as follows:[36]

1. PRECONTOURED CROWNS

These crowns are pre-contoured and also festooned. Some contouring and trimming might be necessary but is usually minimum. The pre-contour is lost and the crown will fit more loosely if the trimming of the crown becomes necessary. They reduce the operating time. However, a little trimming and contouring might be necessary.

2. **PRETRIMMED CROWNS**

These crowns have non-contoured, straight sides to follow a parallel line to the gingival crest. The crowns still need contouring and trimming. These have straight sides and are festooned so that they are parallel to the gingival crest. But they still need contouring as well as trimming.

3. **PREVENEERED CROWNS**

These are the crowns that have resin-based composite to create a more aesthetic posterior crown. They are bonded to the occlusal and buccal surfaces. They are more expensive than the other stainless-steel crowns, require tooth reduction, and allow for only less crimping for crown adaptation.[36]

4. **STAINLESS STEEL CROWNS WITH WHITE FACINGS**

In order to make the steel crowns look more appealing, particularly when front teeth are concerned, there are SSCs with pre-veneered plastic facings. These look much better due to the fact they are "white." But for the white facing to stick to the metal, additional bulk should be added. This ensures that the crown looks rounded or bulbous. Also, note that the white facing can chip off after some time, which in turn, exposes the silver crown beneath. Chipping mostly occurs when kids grind their teeth often. This exerts pressure at the back. [36]

PROS AND CONS OF STAINLESS-STEEL CROWNS

Pros:

- The best option when a temporary fix is needed

- Not very expensive

- Works well on children

- Protects the entire tooth from decay by covering it fully

- They do not require many dental visits to be installed

Cons:

- Not suitable as a permanent fix

- Does not blend in with the rest of your teeth

CHAPTER XIII

COMPOSITE STRIP CROWNS

They are used primarily on anterior teeth. It is applied using a hardening composite and a clear plastic form of mold.Although these materials provide an aesthetic restoration, they are also susceptible to fracture, because the hardening composite inside composite strip crown forms must adhere to dentin and enamel, their placement is sensitive to hemorrhage and moisture

The bonded resin composite strip crown1 is perhaps the most esthetic of all the restorations available to the clinician for the treatment of severely decayed primary incisors. However, strip crowns are also the most technique-sensitive and may be difficult to place. The purpose of this step-by-step technique article is to present some simple clinical tips to assist the clinician in achieving an esthetic and superior outcome.[37]

III. POLYCARBONATE CROWNS

Although these crowns have been available to clinicians for a few years now, owing to the initial published reports pertaining to its retention capabilities, it never got its due recognition. Kudos ™ -Temporary Pediatric Crowns, is a crown that is easy to use and handle along with considerably reducing the chair side working time thereby overcoming the difficulties reported so far pertaining to placement and retention. They are available as both individual as well as full arch crown and bridge both for the maxillary and mandibular anterior and posterior teeth, respectively.

This is a newer generation of Pediatric polycarbonate crowns, which is more clinician friendly and esthetically acceptable. The material is flexible, easily adaptable, and reduces the chair side placement time considerably.[38]

Advantages

- Esthetically acceptable
- Less chair side time

- Improved retention
- Flexible
- Better adaptability

Disadvantages

- Breakages
- Dislodgement
- Discoloration

Placement technique

A through assessment of the case has to be carried out with regards to availability of crown structure, over jet, overbite, habits, infections, and so forth.

Once the assessment is completed, appropriate crown selection is done with care taken to determine the overall fit of the crown over the tooth.

The tooth to be restored is then prepared first mesiodistally followed by incisal reduction, leaving a featheredge margin. Care should be taken to prepare the tooth minimally.

A trial fit is carried out to check for proper fit, marginal adaptability, overall coverage, occlusal interference, and mesiodistal width.

Necessary adjustments are made to the polycarbonate crown, using either a crown cutting scissors or a trimming stone. Care must be taken to seat the crowns on to the prepared margins.

After the final fit is done, the crown is relined using a self-cure acrylic resin. The advantage of this type of relining technique is that the resin chemically bonds to the polycarbonate crowns. By priming the inside of the relined crown, it can be bonded to the tooth using composite resin or glass ionomer cement.

After the complete set of the reline material, the margins are trimmed and finished and the crown is cemented using a luting cement or composite resin.

The firmness of the crown allows it to serve as a provisional crown restoration up to several months/years to protect the patient's teeth from trauma.[39][40]

CASE REPORT -1

A male patient (aged 4 years) reported with a complaint of discolored restoration in the upper front teeth. Clinical examination revealed the presence of discolored composite restoration in 51 and 61. The parent gave a history of trauma and subsequent pulp therapy in 51. Owing to the unesthetic nature of the restoration, the parents wanted a crown restoration to be done on the affected teeth. The patient was carefully assessed according the parameters required for restoration using the polycarbonate crown. Once the parameters were found to be satisfactory, it was decided to restore the discolored teeth. Complete removal of the old restorative material and secondary decay below the restoration was carried out followed by restoration with polycarbonate crown . The patient has been under periodic clinical evaluation every 6 months for the last 18 months and the crowns have been found to be intact.[41]

CASE REPORT- 2

A male patient (aged 3 years 10 months) reported with a chief complaint of decayed front teeth. The main complaint of the parent was the aversion of the child toward dental treatment. The child was unwilling to have his dental examination. As the child was uncooperative, the treatment was carried out under general anesthesia after obtaining all medical clearances and signed informed consent from the parents. Complete caries excavation was performed on 51, 51, 61, and 62 followed by preparation of the teeth, and polycarbonate crown and bridge was cemented in place. The postoperative healing was uneventful and the patient is under periodic clinical evaluation since past 2 years.[42]

CHAPTER XIV

RESIN VENEER CROWNS

Resin Veneered Pediatric Stainless Steel Crowns

Resin Veneered Pediatric Crowns are made with a stainless steel crown base but with a veneer front. This solves both purposes which was initially not met by the stainless steel crowns - the issue of aesthetics. The Resin veneer mix is used to create a natural tooth-like appearance which makes it easy to blend in with the rest of the teeth and therefore makes it look very aesthetically pleasing. This type of crown can easily be preferred for making anterior crowns as well.

The pros with Resin Pre veneered stainless steel crowns apart from its looks is that it also has high resistance towards corrosion and they are insensitive to hemorrhage. This makes the placement of these kinds of crowns easier. They are very durable and can last almost as long as Stainless steel crowns and definitely longer than any other tooth- like material crown as well.[43]

The cons when it comes to Resin Pre Veneered Stainless Steel crown is the fact that the resin veneer part may sometimes chip. Although this is rare, one needs to be precautionary as the resin part is not as strong as the underlying steel part and therefore much caution needs to be exercised.

Another con is the fact that it cannot be easily contoured or trimmed due to its limited crimping ability as a structure. In such a scenario, more of the natural tooth may have to be removed to make space for this kind of a crown. They are also quite expensive and can be more expensive than other kinds of crowns as well. But they are thankfully covered under many medical policies which is a bright side.[44]

They may require some extra attention in terms of biting force, cleanliness and regular maintenance. Given the cost, children will need to be trained on carefully handling the crown and taught to be careful with the way they chew or bite down on hard things to prevent the resin from chipping.

They are less sensitive to hemorrhage and moisture during placement, their limited crimp ability requires a greater removal of tooth structure. Resin veneered crowns are typically more expensive than stainless steel, composite strip and polycarbonate crowns.[44]

CHAPTER XV

ZIRCONIA CERAMIC CROWNS

Zirconia Crowns are one of the most natural looking solutions to all aesthetic crown related issues. They are perfect for anterior crowns and can easily blend with the rest of the natural teeth with ease. The best part about zirconia crowns is that not only are they aesthetically pleasing, they are also exceptionally strong. They can be used for both posterior and anterior crowns and can prove to be excellent in terms of durability and reliability.

They can last for a really long time and unlike resin veneer crowns, there is no fear of chipping or wearing down. They are very low maintenance and can last up until the permanent teeth show up.

The only cons with regards to Zirconia crowns is that they are quite expensive and may also be one of the most expensive options for crowns in the market. This may make not much sense since the child will soon have their permanent teeth and therefore seem like a dead investment.[45]

Another con is that they are not very easy to contour or trim based on the size of the primary tooth, therefore the procedure to fit the crown may actually be longer and more tedious. It needs to be done from a place that specialises in these kinds of procedures.

Apart from these cons, zirconia is absolutely safe since it is a bioceramic material made often from Zirconium oxide and Yttrium oxide. They may also sometimes contain a layer of porcelain on their outer surface for enhanced strength and appeal.

Zirconia crowns for primary teeth are in high demand from parents who seek more esthetically pleasant dental restorations for their children. Research has been undertaken to compare the properties of zirconia crowns for primary teeth with other similar restorations such as stainless-steel crowns. The zirconia crowns require more tooth structure reduction to accomplish better adaptation. Pulpal exposure and postoperative complications also have been noted during the preparation for zirconia crowns [46]. Even with the variety of companies and esthetic demands, zirconia crowns are considered to be expensive when compared to other treatment alternatives [46,47].

One of the important parameters to assess in a crown is its effect on gingival and periodontal health. An ideal material for a crown would have no plaque accumulation on the surface. Different materials used for crowns may have different properties leading to different plaque accumulation amounts. Other factors such as types of cements also may affect periodontal health. In this review, we found that most of the included studies found that zirconia crowns had significantly lower levels of plaque accumulation, especially when compared to resin-coated crowns [47]. This could be due to the surface properties of zirconia including its superior hardness. This makes them resistant to scratches and they may have a shiny, smooth polished surface. Another reason could be the low surface energy of zirconia crowns which may lead to low plaque and bacterial adhesion. Although, if the plaque accumulated on the surfaces, it was reported to be thinner than the plaque on stainless steel crowns. This is due to the smoother surfaces and margins of zirconia crowns unlike stainless steel crowns or strip crowns which require a customization and recontouring before cementation. The recontouring or adjustments may create irregularities on surfaces and margins, favoring the accumulation of plaque and affecting periodontal health. Therefore, zirconia is being used for a variety of applications such as implants [48]

CHAPTER XVI

DENTAL IMPLANTS IN PEDIATRIC DENTISTRY

I. DENTLAL IMPLANTS

Dental implant is defined as a prosthetic device made up of alloplastic material implanted into the oral tissue under the mucosal or periosteal layer, and on or within the bone to provide retention and support for a fixed or removable prosthesis".

Children and adolescents are seen to manifest anodontia, congenitally missing teeth as well as teeth loss due to trauma.

In these cases, the degree of hypodontia can bring about psychological stress in the child and proper oral rehabilitation of the child is required before skeletal and dental maturation. Here, removable prosthesis is often the treatment of choice. However, it may lead to increase progression rate of caries, residual alveolar ridge resorption, and complications of the periodontium .Shaw reported that the dramatic changes in growth and development occurring in infancy and early childhood were not conducive to the maintenance of implants.[45] According to Dietschl and Schatz" and Mackie and Quayle, implants in children younger than 16 to 18 years must not be placed since adjacent alveolar growth will render them infraoccluded.[45],[46] Bergendal et al stated that implants placement must be delayed upto the point when growth is almost complete, except for rare cases of total aplasia, as in ectodermal dysplasia. [47 The use of implants in adolescents is uncommon because the dental surgeon is concerned about maxillary and mandibular "growth spurts". If he follows the indications and ideal timing of placement of implants, predicting their success will not be a problem for him. If the implant placement protocol in adolescents is followed, they can be used more routinely. Therefore, the aim of this review is to throw light upon the use of dental implants in children, adolescents and young adults to discuss its role in oral rehabilitation of children with partial or complete anadontia and also to bring out the role of dental implants in some special cases where dental implant placement might be the treatment of choice in the near future.

SCOPE OF DENTAL IMPLANTS IN PEDIATRIC DENTISTRY

Implant popularity as a treatment modality in adults is tremendous. In case of adults the amount of research being carried out is extensive, however, the treatment planning and execution of implant placement in children and adolescents is still in its infancy. In partially edentulous cases, long-term success of dental implants has been responsible for other clinicians to broaden the use of implants to adolescents in whom teeth are missing due to trauma or agenesis.. Anodontia either primary or acquired occasionally creates the opportunity for the use of dental implants[.48] In the absence of maxillary teeth, the maxilla will remain underdeveloped both sagittally and vertically as the alveolar ridges will not develop. In contrast, the mandibular growth is not dependent on the presence of teeth. Therefore, disproportionate relationship between two jaws will tend to occur in the presence of hypodontia or anodontia resulting in class III development as growth occurs throughout the normal growth period. Furthermore, physiological and psychological factors increase the pressure to start early treatment.[48] According to World Health Organization –young people between the age of 10 years and 19 years are termed adolescents.[49] However, in adolescents the use of implants differs significantly from adults. Because a variety of changes occur in the dentition and jaws of the adolescent, special importance has to be given to the growth of the child.

IMPLANTS IN GROWING BONE

Placement of implants in children and adolescents has always been controversial. Few researchers advocate their use in this group of patients and a few others strictly contraindicate their usage. Bjork[50],[51] conducted one of the pioneering studies concerning growth patterns of the dental arches and replicating the implant insertion . For longitudinal cephalometric studies,he implanted 0.5 mm × 1.5 mm. tantalum pins in the jaws of growing children as stable landmarks. Although most pins were stable, pins affected by growth were not. The pins were also displaced by orthodontic tooth movement. Nearly all the pins placed in the resorptive areas like the anterior mandibular ramus, were lost and had to be replaced. In addition, pins placed in areas of appositional bone growth gradually became embedded. Oesterle et al,[52] and Brahim[53] compared dental implants to ankylosed primary teeth. With lack of alveolar growth and dental eruption, an osseointegrated implant behaves much like an ankylosed primary tooth. These authors proposed that implants placed in the posterior maxilla in children may become buried to the point that the apical portion may become exposed as the nasal and antral floor remodel. Odman et al, [54] recommended that implants should not be placed posterior to the canines during active growth. In children with strong rotational pattern, posterior teeth undergo continued eruption, along with continued alveolar bone growth to maintain the occlusal plane, possibly causing implants to become deeply buried within the mandibular alveolar process.[55]

INDICATIONS AND CONTRAINDICATIONS OF PLACING DENTAL IMPLANTS IN PEDIATRIC DENTAL PATIENTS

Indications for use of implants in adolescents

1. Pediatric patients with ectodermal dysplasia (1988 National Institute of Health Consensus Development Conference on Dental Implants at Bethesda)
2. Implants combined with bone grafting in patients with cleft of the alveolus and palate.

Child and adolescents having anodontia, partial anodontia, congenitally missing teeth, teeth lost as a result of trauma.

Contra-indications for the use of dental implants

1. **Pre -pubertal age group.**
2. **Individual with pre pubertal growth spurt.**
3. **Inadequate mesiodistal space.**

INDICATORS OF COMPLETION OF GROWTH

Completion of growth in an individual is not estimated by chronological age alone. Studying tracings of serial cephalometric radiographs taken at least 6 months apart by superimposing is probably the most reliable method, though it requires a lot of time and irradiation and may unnecessarily delay implant insertion. Waiting for implant insertion until no growth change is seen over a period of 1 year is ideal. Skeletal growth status can be accurately appraised by comparing a conventional hand and wrist radiograph against a standardized atlas of hand and the wrist bone development. After maximum growth velocity is completed, capping of the middle phalanges of the third finger (MP3cap) usually occurs and it is an indication of deceleration in the pubertal growth spurt.On completion of pubertal growth spurt,impant placement can be considered although some risks still exist. Adult level of skeletal growth is attained when epiphysis of the radius fuses and forms a bony union with the diaphysis. This is the considered the safest time to place a solitary implant.

CHOOSING A PROPER IMPLANT INSERTION AGE

The possibility exists to place implants even before the pubertal growth spurt in cases of severe anodontia or oligodontia in the mandible, since in this patient group few growth changes occur in the anterior mandibular region after the age of 5-6 years, especially because of the absence of teeth.

For the maxilla, it is suggested to wait until after the growth spurt.

During the consensus meeting in 1995 it was decided that implant placement in adolescents preferably should be postponed until the end of the craniofacial/skeletal growth.

Cronin et al. [56] observed that if implants are placed during active growth, they may be displaced or malpositioned by continued growth and may require removal and replacement. Implants placed after age 15 for girls and age 18 for boys have the most predictable prognosis. Implants placed before these ages may not be permanent and may have to be reimplanted. [56.]

In summary, psychological benefits may be associated with using implants to support an oral prosthesis in the jaws of a teenage child with many missing teeth. However clinical research has not demonstrated compelling reasons to place implants in pre teenage children to support an oral prosthesis. Carefully controlled prospective clinical studies are needed to determine the efficacy and effectiveness of the use of implants in children and young adults.[57].

II. MINI-IMPLANTS IN PEDIATRIC DENTISTRY

What is mini implants? A mini-implant is a miniature sized titanium implant that acts like the root a of tooth. Mini implants were first developed by Dr Victor I Sendax of Newyork in the early 1985. Bulard added single one piece ball design. They have a diameter of 1.8mm to 2.7, they are available in multiple tip, thread, body and head.[58]

Thread designs vary from thin to thick and thread spacing is also variable. Square, rectangular or o- ball heads are common. Height and anatomic structures of the bone determine the length, shape, and thickness of mini-implants

Parts of mini implants

- Head – This part of the mini-implant is exposed to the oral environment. is mainly designed to receive attachments like elastics or wires

- Neck – the connecting part between head and body It is of three different heights such as 1mm, 2mm and 3mm for accommodating different soft- tissue thickness at different implants sites.
- Body of the implant is parallel. It is either of self-drilling or self-tapping type. It has threads and grooves for better interlocking of the mini-implant to the bone

Comparison of Mini implants with conventional implants

Mini implants are made of one part whereas conventional implants consist of two parts(the implant and the abutment). Mini implants have one piece titanium screw with a ball shaped head for denture stabilization or square prosthetic head for fixed applications instead of the classic abutment. Mini implants protruded over the gingival surface when they are placed into the bone whereas conventional implants are placed under the gingival .[61]

Size: Mini implants are smaller in size which makes them ideal for replacing smaller teeth in areas where space is limited as well as for securing full or partial dentures whereas conventional implants are more widely used when replacing larger teeth or for securing a bridge of teeth.

Durability-Both types of implants are made from highgrade titanium alloy. Strength of an implant is due to the length of the post or screw rather than the diameter. Even though mini implants are narrower than conventional implants, the length of the post is comparable to conventional implants. Mini implants are less able to withstand substantial chewing forces when compared to conventional implants and for this reason conventional implants tend to be used when replacing molars

Price: Due to their smaller size and the straight forward nature of the surgery to place them, mini implants are more affordable than conventional implants.

Longevity and Success of Treatment: A properly placed and well-maintained conventional dental implant has a very high rate of success and can last for decades or even for life. Mini implants are a much more recent innovation and fewer studies have been conducted into their success [62]

Mini implant in children: Mini implants as a prosthetic replacement gives a psychological advantage to the child as it provides a feeling of his own teeth, the relatively small diameter allows the fixture to be placed even in the presence of transverse bone loss, the mini-implants have minimal osseointegration and, consequently, allow the volumes of soft and bone tissues to be maintained until growth is complete , their removal is non traumatic and not associated with any further deficit

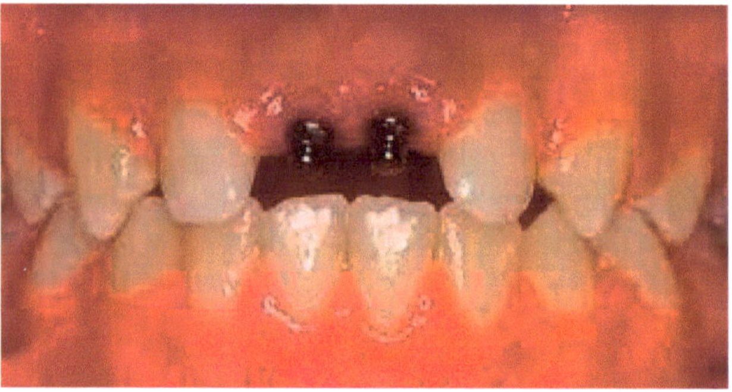

Fig no 19

The miniscrew stimulates the alveolar ridge and thus helps prevent ridge atrophy, and it prevents the adjacent roots from drifting into the edentulous space.Sousa de Oliveira et al. has shown that artificial tooth supporting orthodontic implants can be successfully used to restore missing permanent teeth in children [63](fig.19)

Another study showed that mini-implants have no remarkable harm on the bone after immediate loading directly after surgery [63] The simplicity of insertion of mini implants, the lack of a recovery period and their low cost, compared with conventional implants, make them extremely suitable for temporary prosthetic treatment in children during the period of jaw bone growth [62][63]

This technique is intended to temporarily satisfy the esthetic needs of the patient and can be used as a space maintainer option until the general growth of the patient is complete and the patient is monetarily ready to undergo further restorative treatment.[64]

Contraindication

- Uncontrolled diabetes
- Clotting disorders
- Anticoagulant therapy like heparin , antiplatelet drugs
- Metabolic bone disease
- Chemotherapy or radiation therapy
- Chronic periodontal inflammation
- Insufficient soft tissue coverage
- Metabolic or systemic disorders associated with wound and/or bone healing
- Use of pharmaceuticals that inhibit or alter natural bone remodeling like bisphosphate
- Disorders inhibiting patient ability to maintain adequate daily oral hygiene
- Uncontrolled parafunctional habits

An edentulous smile might look appealing in an infant but its persistence is a serious cause of concern for the parents and the child. Mini-implant is becoming promising alternative to crown anchorage in the anterior region, especially in oral rehabilitation of growing patient due to its simple ways to use, versatility and great biocompatibility. It provides good aesthetic and functional results which improves the child's quality of life, social integration and increases the self-esteem.[64]

CHAPTER XVII

THE SPACE MAINTAINERS

Space Maintenance-

It is defined as the process of maintaining a space in a given arch previously occupied by a tooth or a group of teeth. [65]

- **Space Maintainer-** it is a fixed or removable appliance designed to preserve the space created by the premature loss of a primary tooth or a group of teeth.[65]

SPACE LOSS ANTERIOR SEGMENT-

a. For Space Maintenance: Replacement is not required for space maintenance because there is no net loss of space in anterior segment rather some rearrangement of incisors may occur that does not affect arch length.
b. Function: Poor masticatory function serves as a strong reason for the incisor replacement. It can occur in two segments-
c. Speech- A space maintainer must be given for speech development.
d. Aesthetics- Most valid reason for incisor replacement.
e. Prevention of social trauma for child.

POSTERIOR SEGMENT

Replacement is mainly done for the space maintenance because there are more chances of mesial drift in posteriors. Various factors which has to be taken into consideration are-

- Age of the patient
- Status of occlusion
- Presence or absence of abnormal perioral muscle habits.[65]

FACTORS AFFECTING PLANNING FOR SPACE MAINTAINERS

1. Time Elapsed since loss: Most of the space loss usually takes place during the first 6 months after the primary tooth is lost. it is best to insert an appliance as soon as possible after the extraction.
2. Eruption Status of the Adjacent Teeth: More space loss is likely to occur if teeth are actively erupting adjacent to the area left by the premature loss of the primary tooth.[65]
3. Amount of Bone Coverage Over the Tooth : 1mm of bone resorbs in 4 to 5 months and so if the bone is present over the succedaneous tooth it is an indication for space maintainer.
4. Sequence of eruption of teeth: Observe the relationship of developing & erupting teeth adjacent to the space created by the untimely loss of a tooth.
5. 5.Congenital absence of permanent tooth
6. Dental Age of Patient-It is the age calculated according to the last tooth erupted in oral cavity in normal eruption sequence.
7. Sequence of Eruption-Knowledge of usual eruption sequence is important.
8. Abnormal Oral Habits-They will exert abnormal pressure on dental arches and so may influence the type and planning of space maintainer.[66]

IDEAL REQUIREMENTS

1. It should maintain the desired mesiodistal dimension of the space.
2. Should not interfere with the vertical eruption of the adjacent teeth.
3. Provide mesiodistal space opening when required.
4. Should maintain individual functional movement of teeth.
5. Should not endanger the remaining teeth by imposing excessive stresses on them.
6. Should be easily cleaned & not serve as traps for debris.
7. Must not restrict the growth of jaws. [66]

CLASSIFICATIONS

(I) According to Hitchcock-

- Removable, fixed or semifixed
- With bands or without bands
- Functional or non functional
- Active or passive
- Certain combinations of the above

(II) According to Raymond C. Thurow-
- Removable
- Complete arch -Lingual arch -Extra oral anchorage
- Individual tooth

(III) According to Hinrichsen-

1. **Fixed space maintainers**

   Class –I
   (a) Non functional types - Bar type - Loop type
   (b) Functional types - Pontic type - Lingual arch type
   Class-II
   Cantilever type
   - Distal shoe
   - Band & Loop

2. Removable space maintainers
Acrylic partial dentures

Fixed Space Maintainers

I.   BAND AND LOOP SPACE MAINTAINER

I.   LINGUAL ARCH SPACE MAINTAINER

III. NANCE PALATAL ARCH SPACE MAINTAINER

IV. TRANSPALATAL ARCH

V. DISTAL SHOE SPACE MAINTAINER.[67]

ADVANTAGES:

1. Easy manipulation.
2. The bands are used without tooth preparation or with minimum preparation in case of stainless steel crowns.
3. It does not interfere with passive eruption of abutments.
4. The jaw growth is not hampered.
5. The succedaneous permanent teeth are well guided to their positions
6. Masticatory function is restored if pontics are placed.

DISADVANTAGES:

1. Elaborate instrumentation with expert skill is needed.
2. They may result in decalcification of tooth material under the bands.
3. May be harmful to the abutment tooth due to the development of torque forces resulting in appliance breakage.
4. Supraeruption of opposing teeth if pontics are not used.[67]

Removable space maintainer

The removable space maintainers or partial denture maintainers are useful when there is bilateral premature loss of deciduous molars or unilateral loss of multiple deciduous teeth, and the permanent incisors have not yet erupted.

In this case, a lower lingual holding arc is contraindicated due to the likelihood of the mandibular permanent incisors erupting lingual to the wire. Removable space maintainers are avoided, if possible, because of the lack of compliance in younger patient. They are frequently misplaced, lost and broken. Unilateral removable space maintainers should never be used due to their small size and the danger of swallowing.

Its advantages are to maintain the leeway space via incorporation of false teeth and since there are false teeth incorporation into the appliance, occlusal function is restored.

Anterior esthetics can also be restored when there is premature loss of deciduous anterior teeth in conjunction with premature loss of deciduous posterior teeth.[68]

Fixed space maintainers

Fixed appliances are less bulky, easier for patients to accept and manage and require less regular care. Follow-up at appropriate intervals is crucial to the removal of the appliance in accordance with eruption of the permanent successor. They can be classified as unilateral or bilateral, maxillary or mandibular

BAND AND LOOP SPACE MAINTAINER

It is a unilateral, nonfunctional, passive, fixed appliance indicated for space maintenance in the posterior segments.

INDICATIONS:

a. Unilateral loss of the primary first molar before or after eruption of the permanent first molar.

a. Bilateral loss of a primary molar before the eruption of the permanent incisors.

BAND – STAINLESS STEEL MATERIAL

- .LOOP – Stainless steel round 0.036 inch wire.

- DESIGN OF LOOP : The loop should parallel the edentulous ridge 1 mm off the gingival tissue and should rest against the adjacent tooth at the contact point.

- The faciolingual dimension of the loop should be approximately 8 mm.

- This dimension should allow the permanent tooth to erupt freely but not impinge on the buccal mucosa or tongue.

- Soldering the loop to the band
  The loop is stabilized by placing plaster in the anterior region of the loop and then soldering is done using silver solder after the flux is melted or dried.
  The band should be cemented onto a clean, dry abutment tooth with a Glass Ionomer cement.

ADVANTAGES:

1. It is an effective space maintainer for unilateral loss of single tooth in buccal segments.
2. It is economical to make and construction is simple.
3. It takes little chair side time if preformed bands are used.
4. It can be adjusted easily to accommodate the changing dentition.

DISADVANTAGES

1. It is not functional as it does not restore masticatory needs of the replacing tooth.
2. It does not prevent the continued eruption of opposing tooth.
3. Incase of fixed maintainers, decalcification under the bands is a problem.
4. It is more prone to slip gingivally during mastication and get embedded in soft tissue if unnoticed for a long time.
5. It may cause eruption disturbances if distorted.

Modifications

- Crown and loop -Stainless steel crown is used on abutment tooth instead of a band.
- Crown-band and loop: Stainless steel crown is first placed on abutment tooth and then it is banded. • Reverse band and loop – In case of premature loss of primary 2nd molar and the permanent molars have not erupted fully to support a band.

- Band and bar
- Bonded band and loop
- Long band and loop[69][70]

LINGUAL ARCH SPACE MAINTAINER

It is a unilateral, nonfunctional, passive, fixed appliance indicated for space maintenance in the posterior segments.

It is a bilateral, nonfunctional, passive/active, mandibular fixed appliance.

It is the most effective appliance of space maintenance and minor tooth movement in lower arch.

INDICATIONS-

- Bilateral loss of primary molars after eruption of Permanent lower central and lateral incisors.
- Unilateral loss of primary molars after eruption of Permanent lower central and lateral incisors.
- Minor space regaining.
- BAND – STAINLESS STEEL MATERIAL 0.005 INCH IN THICKNESS
- Lingual arch wire- Stainless steel round wire 0.036 inches in diameter.

DESIGN OF WIRE LOOP-

- Arch wire should contact the erupted permanent incisors at cingulum.
- Arch wire should be located 2 mm below the gingival margin in the posterior tooth region to prevent distortion under masticatory forces.
- Should be located 1 -2 mm lingual to posterior teeth to permit satisfactory eruption of premolar in buccolingual plane.
- Arch wire should meet the band at mesiolingual cusp and soldered at middle third of band to avoid occlusal interference.

ADVANTAGES

1. It is an excellent source of anchorage because it incorporates resistance of several teeth.

2. It allows free individual movement of teeth while maintaining space in desired areas.
3. It serves as a space maintainer for more than one succedaneous tooth in the arch.

DISADVANTAGES

1. Prolonged use may cause decalcification of the tooth.
2. The arch wire may become embedded into the soft tissues. This seems to occur more often in patients with poor oral hygiene.
3. The wire may be distorted by masticatory forces and move teeth into undesirable positions.

Modifications-

- Hotz lingual arch - U loop used for space regaining.
- Omega bends - In canine region to prevent interference.[69].

NANCE PALATAL ARCH SPACE MAINTAINER

Bilateral, nonfunctional, passive, maxillary fixed appliance that does not contact the anterior teeth, but approximates the anterior palate via an acrylic button

- Acrylic button that contacts the palatal tissues which provides resistance to the anterior movement of posterior teeth.[67]

INDICATIONS-

- Maintain maxillary first permanent molar position when there is bilateral premature loss of primary teeth with no loss of space in arch.
- Combined with habit breaking appliance.
- BAND – STAINLESS STEEL MATERIAL 0.005 INCH IN THICKNESS
- PALATAL WIRE -Stainless steel round wire 0.036 inches in thickness .[71]

DESIGN OF THE WIRE LOOP-

- Arch wire extends anteriorly without touching against surface of primary molar, as successor bicuspids are broader buccolingually, wire could deflect from their natural position
- At rugae area u shaped bend should be incorporated in wire (approx. 1-2 mm away form the soft tissue)
- Acrylic button 0.5 in diameter is placed on the descending portion of palatal vault 1-2 mm below incisive papilla.

Advantage

- Maxillary arch stabilizing.

Disadvantages-

- May cause tissue hyperplasia
- .Irritation to palatal tissues.
- Pressure effects.
- Cannot be used in patients allergic to acrylic.[72]

TRANSPALATAL ARCH fig.20)

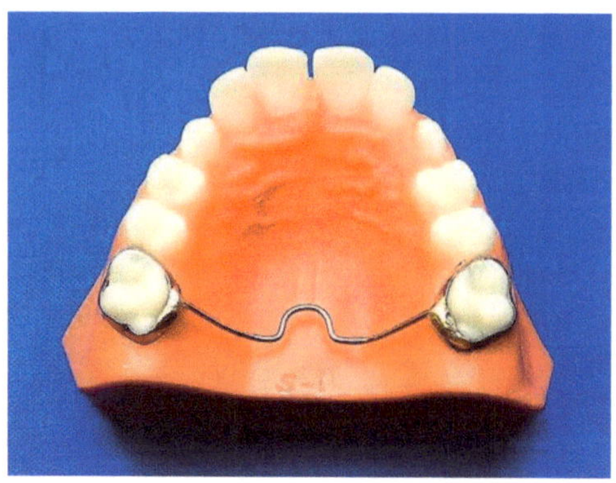

Fig no 20

INDICATIONS –

- When one side of the arch is intact and several primary teeth on the other side are missing.
- Appliance is designed to prevent molars from rotation around the palatal roots.
- In arch expansion.
- BAND – STAINLESS STEEL MATERIAL 0.005 INCH IN THICKNESS
- PALATAL WIRE -Stainless steel round wire 0.036 inches in thick

DESIGN OF THE WIRE LOOP

- Arch wire runs directly across the palatal vault avoiding contact with soft tissue
- U shaped bend must be given in middle of palate.
- As the arch wire approaches mesial part of palatal surface of the band, the wire should be bent to distal part of band to assure better joint. [73]
-

Advantages

- Used in multiple unilateral loss
- Can be used for expansion

Disadvantages

- Rotation of molars.
- Both molars may tip together

DISTAL SHOE SPACE MAINTAINER

The distal shoe appliance is also called as the intra alveolar appliance.

- The distal root surface of the second primary molar provides a guide for the unerupted first permanent molar.

- When the second primary molar is removed prior to the eruption of the first permanent molar, the intra alveolar appliance provides greater control of the path of eruption of the unerupted tooth and prevents undesirable mesial migration.

INDICATION

It is indicated when the second primary molar is extracted or lost before eruption of first permanent molar.

CONTRAINDICATIONS

1. Inadequate abutments due to multiple loss of teeth.
2. Poor oral hygiene due to lack of parent or patient cooperation.
3. Medically compromised patients like patients with congenital heart diseases, juvenile diabetics, history of rheumatic fever.
4. Congenitally missing first permanent molar. [74]

Construction

- Using first primary molar as abutment, the stainless-steel band is adapted. If morphology of the tooth does not permit easy placement and adaptation of band then the tooth is prepared for stainless steel crown which is carefully contoured and cemented.
- The stainless steel crown provides a desirable contour for the placement of stainless steel band.
- The band is placed over the stainless steel crown or abutment tooth. An alginate impression is made, the band is removed and placed in the impression and a stone model is prepared.
- Construction of loop-The tissue bearing loop is then contoured with a 0.040 inch wire extending distally and into the prepared opening on the model. The free ends of the loop are soldered to the band or directly to the stainless-steel crown.
- Before final placement of the space maintainer in the mouth, a intra oral radiograph is taken to determine whether the tissue extension of the appliance is in proper relationship with the unerupted 1st permanent molar.[75]

CHAPTER XVIII

MONITORING

Once the space maintainer has been placed, it may take the child a few days to get accustomed to wearing the appliance whether it is removable or fixed. The parents should be carefully monitoring the child to make sure is wearing it, if the maintainer is removable and ensure he is following a proper oral hygiene routine.

The dentist should review with the child and parent the proper ways to clean the space maintainer thoroughly in order to keep the gum tissue healthy and free of dental plaque. Proper instruction for tooth brushing and flossing should be considered for improved oral hygiene

If the space maintainer is fixed, it will be important to avoid chewy, gum or candy, which may loosen or get caught on the appliance. Also, the space maintainer should not be pressed or pushed with the tongue or fingers, because it could loosen or bend the appliance. The child should be seen by the dentist regularly to make sure that the development and growth of the new tooth or teeth is on track and following the path that the space maintainer has allowed. Once the permanent tooth or teeth are growing in properly, the space maintainer can be removed.

CHAPTER XIX

CONCLUSION

The loss of a tooth could be caused by trauma, decay process or can be genetic. This loss causes functional, aesthetic as well as psychological problems. To overcome these adverse consequences for the child, the dentist has several prosthetic therapeutic devices, whether fixed or removable. Nowadays, most dentists do not treat this dental loss as they should. Although pediatric prosthesis is not yet rooted in the habits of dentist's daily practice, it remains essential in order to avoid problems resulting from a big loss of teeth.

Often, the parents do not realize the importance to cap or replace a tooth that will be soon exfoliated or replaced by a permanent tooth; this is why it is very important to inform the patient and their parents about the risks of a lack of treatment.

The interest of the child must be the first motivation of the dentist. Like any dental treatment, prosthetic treatment plans in children follow a rational therapeutic approach taking into consideration the patient's motivation as well as that of his parents, oral hygiene ant the clinical situation.

Finally, all types of pedodontics treatment require a regular monitoring and control.

CHAPTER XX

REFERENCES

1. Vulićević Z, Beloica M, Kosanović D, Radović I, Juloski J, Ivanović D. Prosthetics in paediatric dentistry. Balkan Journal of Dental Medicine. 2017;21(2):78-82.
2. Lindblad-Toh K, Garber M, Zuk O, Lin MF, Parker BJ, Washietl S, Kheradpour P, Ernst J, Jordan G, Mauceli E, Ward LD. A high-resolution map of human evolutionary constraint using 29 mammals. Nature. 2011 Oct;478(7370):476- 82.
3. Hoffding J, Kisling E. Premature loss of primary teeth: part I, its overall effect on occlusion and space in the permanent dentition. ASDC journal of dentistry for children. 1978 Jul 1;45(4):279-83.
4. Bidra AS, Martin JW, Feldman E. Complete denture prosthodontics in children with ectodermal dysplasia: review of principles and techniques. Compendium of continuing education in dentistry (Jamesburg, NJ: 1995). 2010 Jul 1;31(6):426-33.
5. Schnoering G. Thérapeutiques de la première molaire permanente: considérations et répercussions vis-à-vis de l'ancrage orthodontique: élaboration d'un guide clinique à l'attention de l'omnipraticien (Doctoral dissertation, Université de Lorraine)
6. Bassil J. *Prosthetic management of deciduous teeth* (Doctoral dissertation, [sn]).
7. Trivedi BD, Bhatia R. Complete and removable partial prosthesis for a child with hypohidrotic ectodermal dysplasia. Int J Clin Pediatr Dent. 2013 Jan;6(1):71-4. doi: 10.5005/jp-journals-10005-1192. Epub 2013 Apr 26..
8. Sweet C.A. A classification and treatment for traumatized anterior teeth. ASDC J Dent. Child., 1955; 22: 144-9. 2.
9. Shobha Tandon. Text book of Pedodontics. 2nd edition, India: Paras, 2009.
10. Bennett D.T. Traumatized anterior teeth assessing the injury and principle of treatment. Br. Dent. J., 1963; 115: 309- 11. 4.

11. Enrique Basrani. Fractures of the teeth. 4 th edition, Lea & Febiger, Elsivier, Mosby, 1982. 5.

12. Hargreaves A, Craig W, Needleman L. The management of traumatized anterior teeth of children; 2nd edition, Churchill Livingstone, 1981.

13. Network FA. The mystery of declining tooth decay. Nature. 1986 Jul 10;332:125-9.

14. Marwah N. Textbook of pediatric dentistry. JP Medical Ltd; 2018 Oct 31.

15. Muthu MS, Kumar S. Pediatric dentistry. Elsevier Health Sciences; 2019 Mar 15.

16. Dosumu OO, Ogunrinde JT, Bamigboye SA. Knowledge of consequences of missing teeth in patients attending prosthetic clinic in uCh Ibadan. Annals of Ibadan postgraduate medicine. 2014 Sep 15;12(1):42-8.

17. Innes NP, Ricketts D, Chong LY, Keightley AJ, Lamont T, Santamaria RM. Preformed crowns for decayed primary molar teeth. Cochrane Database Syst Rev, 2015;12:CD005512.

18. Engel RJ. Chrome steel as used in children's dentistry. Chron Omaha Dist Dent Soc, 1950;13:255-258

19. Noble J, Ahing SI, Karaiskos NE, Wiltshire WA. Nickel allergy and orthodontics, a review and report of two cases. Br Dent J, 2008:204:297-300.

20. Prabhakar AR, Yavagal CM, Chakraborty A, Sugandhan S. Finite element stress analysis of stainless steel crowns. J Indian Soc Pedod Prev Dent, 2015;33:183-191.

21. . Bhalla G, Agrawal KK, Chand P, Singh K, Singh BP, Goel P et al. Effect of Complete Dentures on Craniofacial Growth of an Ectodermal Dysplasia Patient: A Clinical Report. J Prosthodont, 2013;22:495-500.

22. Bidaki M, Moghadam NC, Takhtdar M, Kamareh S, Kordafshari B. Complete denture prosthodontics in children with ectodermal dysplasia: systematic review from case reports and case series reports. Journal of International Pharmaceutical Research. 2019;46:181-4.

23. Maroulakos G, Artopoulou II, Angelopoulou MV, Emmanouil D. Removable partial dentures vs overdentures in children with ectodermal dysplasia: two case reports. European archives of paediatric dentistry. 2016 Jun;17(3):205-10.

24. Chung YS, Lee NY, Lee SH. Removable flexible denture for child with loss of multiple teeth: a case report. JOURNAL OF THE KOREAN ACADEMY OF PEDTATRIC DENTISTRY. 2007;34(3):513-8.

25. Imirzalioglu P, Uckan S, Haydar SG. Surgical and prosthodontic treatment alternatives for children and adolescents with ectodermal dysplasia: a clinical report. The Journal of prosthetic dentistry. 2002 Dec 1;88(6):569-72.

26. Rodd HD, Atkin JM. Denture satisfaction and clinical performance in a paediatric population. International Journal of Paediatric Dentistry. 2000 Mar;10(1):27-37.

27. Antonescu E. Removable partial denture in special clinical conditions. Revista Medico-chirurgicala a Societatii de Medici si Naturalisti din Iasi. 1997 Jul 1;101(3-4):161-5.

28. Trivedi BD, Bhatia R. Complete and removable partial prosthesis for a child with hypohidrotic ectodermal dysplasia. International Journal of Clinical Pediatric Dentistry. 2013 Jan;6(1):71.

29. Ribeiro DG, Pavarina AC, Giampaolo ET, Machado AL, Jorge JH, Garcia PP. Effect of oral hygiene education and motivation on removable partial denture wearers: longitudinal study. Gerodontology. 2009 Jun;26(2):150-6.

30. Cankaya ZT, YURKADOS A, Kalabay PG. The association between denture care and oral hygiene habits, oral hygiene knowledge and periodontal status of geriatric patients wearing removable partial dentures. European oral research. 2020 Jan 1;54(1):9-15.

31. Lindh T, Dahlgren S, Gunnarsson K, Josefsson T, Nilson H, Wilhelmsson P, Gunne J. Tooth-implant supported fixed prostheses: a retrospective multicenter study. International Journal of Prosthodontics. 2001 Jul 1;14(4).

32. Seale NS. The use of stainless-steel crowns. Pediatric Dentistry. 2002 Sep 1;24(5):501-5.

33. Seale NS, Randall R. The use of stainless-steel crowns: a systematic literature review. Pediatric dentistry. 2015 Apr 15;37(2):145-60.

34. Seale NS, Randall R. The use of stainless-steel crowns: a systematic literature review. Pediatric dentistry. 2015 Apr 15;37(2):120-30.

35. Waggoner WF, Cohen H. Failure strength of four veneered primary stainless- steel crowns. Pediatric dentistry. 1995 Jan 1;17(1):36-40.

36. Beattie S, Taskonak B, Jones J, Chin J, Sanders B, Tomlin A, Weddell J. Fracture resistance of 3 types of primary esthetic stainless-steel crowns. J Can Dent Assoc. 2011 Jan 1;77(77):b90.

37. Holsinger DM, Wells MH, Scarbecz M, Donaldson M. Clinical evaluation and parental satisfaction with pediatric zirconia anterior crowns.

Pediatric dentistry. 2016 Jun 15;38(3):192-7.

38. Weinberger SJ. Treatment modalities for primary incisors. J Can Dent Assoc 1989;55:807-12. Back to cited text no. 2

39. Hartmann CR. The open-face stainless steel crown: An esthetic technique. ASDC J Dent Child 1983;50:31-3. Back to cited text no. 3

40. Helpin ML. The open - face steel crown restoration in children. ASDC J Dent Child 1983;50:34-8. Back to cited text no. 4

41. Webber DL, Epstein NB, Wong JW, Tsamtsouris A. A Method of restoring primary anterior teeth with the aid of celluloid crown form and composite resins. Pediatric Dent 1979;1:244-6. Back to cited text no. 5

42. Pollard MA, Curzon JA, Fenlon WL. Restoration of decayed primary incisors using strip crowns. Dent Update 1991;18:150-2

43. William V, Messer LB, Burrow MF. Molar incisor hypomineralization: review and recommendations for clinical management. Pediatric dentistry. 2006 May 1;28(3):224-32.

44. Innes NP, Ricketts D, Chong LY, Keightley AJ, Lamont T, Santamaria RM. Preformed crowns for decayed primary molar teeth. Cochrane Database of Systematic Reviews. 2015(12).

45. 5. Dietschi D, Schatz JP. Current restorative modalities for young patients with missing anterior teeth. Pediatric Dentistry.1997; 28:231-240.

46. Mackie IC, Quaylc AA. Implants in children: A case report. Endodontic Dental Traumatology. 1993;9:124- 126.

47. Bergendal B, Bergendai T, Hailonsten AL, Koch G, Kuroi J, Kvint S. A multidisciplinary approach to oral rehabilitation with osseointegrated implants in children and adolescents with multiple aplasia. Europian Journal of Orthodontics 1996:18:119-129.

48. Escobar V, Epker BN. Alveolar bone growth in response to endosteal implants in two patients with ectodermal dysplasia. International Journal of Oral and Maxillofacial Surgery. 1998;27:445–7.

49. American Pyschological Association-A Reference for Professionals – Developing Adolescents.

50. Bjork A. Growth of the maxilla in three dimensions as revealed radiographically by the implant method. Br J Orthod 1977;4:53-64.

51. . Bjork A. Variation in the growth pattern of the human mandible. A longitudinal radiographic study by the implant method. J DentRes 1963;42:400

52. Oesterle LJ, Cronin RJ, Jr, Ranly DM. Maxillary implants and the growing patient. International Journal of Oral and Maxillofacial Implants. 1993;8:377– 87.

53. Brahim JS. Dental Implants in children. Oral Maxillofacial Surgery.Dental clinics of North America. 2005;17(4):375-81.

54. Odman J, Gröndahl K, Lekholm U, Thilander B. The effect of osseointegrated implants on the dento-alveolar development. A clinical and radiographic study in growing pigs. European Journal of Orthodontics. 1991; 13:279–86.

55. Westwood RM, Duncan JM. Implants in adolescents: A literature review and case reports. International Journal of Oral Maxillofacial Implants. 1996; 11:750–5.

56. Cronin RJ, Jr, Oesterle LJ, Ranly DM. Mandibular implants and the growing patient. International Journal of Oral and Maxillofacial Implants. 1994;9:55–62

57. Thilander B, Odman J, Gröndahl K, Friberg B. Osseointegrated implants in adolescents. An alternative in replacing missing teeth? European Journal of Orthodontics.1994;16:84– 9

58. Choi R. 2007. Incorporating mini-implants within the general dental practice. Dent Pract Proc Aesth., 19:15.)

59. Costa A., Raffainl M., Melsen B. 1998. Miniscrews as orthodontic anchorage: a preliminary report. The International journal of adult orthodontics and orthognathic surgery., 13(3):201-9.

60. Cronin JR., Oesterle LJ. 1998. Implant use in growing patients. Treatment planning concerns. Dental clinics of North America. Jan;42(1):1-34.

61. de Oliveira NS, Barbosa GLR., Lanza LD., Pretti H. 2017. Prosthetic Rehabilitation of Child Victim of Avulsion of Anterior Teeth with Orthodontic Mini-Implant. Case Rep Dent.; 2017:8905965. [PubMed] [CrossRef] Dimova- Gabrovska M,

62. Dimitrova D, Mitronin VA. 2018. Prosthetic treatment with crowns and implants in children– literature review. Journal of IMAB–Annual Proceeding Scientific Papers., Sep 12;24(3):2166-71.

63. Dwijendra KS., Gheware A, Patil SK, Inchanalkar R, Gugwad S, Kathariya MD. 2015. Experience of Pediatric Patients with Mini-Implants undergoing Orthodontic Treatment. Journal of International Oral Health. Oct 1;7(10):112.

64. Fouziya B., Uthappa MA., Amara D., Tom N., Byrappa S., Sunny K. 2016. Surface modifications of titanium implants–The new, the old, and the never heard of options. Journal of Advanced Clinical and Research Insights. Nov 1;3(6):215-9.

65. Pinkham JR, Casamassimo PS, Fields HW, McTigue DJ, Nowak A. Pediatric dentistry. Infancy through adolescence. 2005 Sep 20;4.

66. Avery DR, McDonald RE. McDonald and avery dentistry for the child and adolescent-E-book. Elsevier Health Sciences; 2010 Apr 8.

67. Laing E, Ashley P, Naini FB, Gill DS. Space maintenance. International journal of paediatric dentistry. 2009 May;19(3):155-62.

68. Kupietzky A. Clinical technique: removable appliance therapy for space maintenance following early loss of primary molars. European Archives of Paediatric Dentistry. 2007 Nov;8(1):30-4.

69. Sharma DS, Srivastava S, Tandon S. Preventive orthodontic approach for functional mandibular shift in early mixed dentition: A case report. Journal of oral biology and craniofacial research. 2019 Apr 1;9(2):209-14.

70. Nayak UA, Sajeev R, Peter J. Band and loop space maintainer-made easy. J Indian Soc Pedod Prev Dent. 2004 Sep 1;22(3):134-6.

71. Kupietzky A, Tal E. The transpalatal arch: an alternative to the Nance appliance for space maintenance. Pediatric dentistry. 2007 May 1;29(3):235-8.

72. Martín-Vacas A, Caleya AM, Gallardo NE. Comparative Analysis of Space Maintenance Using Transpalatal Arch and Nance Button. Journal of Clinical Pediatric Dentistry. 2021;45(2):129-34.

73. Muthu MS, Kumar S. Pediatric dentistry. Elsevier Health Sciences; 2019 Mar 15.

74. Beena JP. Distal Shoe, an Effective Space Maintainer for Premature Loss of Primary Mandibular Second Molar-A Case Report. International Journal of Clinical Preventive Dentistry. 2011;7(4):209-12.

75. Hicks EP. Treatment planning for the distal shoe space maintainer. Dental Clinics of North America. 1973 Jan 1;17(1):135-50.